TUMBLING TIDE

Also by the author

The Raven Tales
The Spark in the Stone
Survival Skills of the North American Indians

TUMBLING TIDE

Population, Petroleum, and Systemic Collapse

Peter Goodchild

INSOMNIAC PRESS

Library and Archives Canada Cataloguing in Publication

Goodchild, Peter, 1949-, author
Tumbling tide : population, petroleum, and systemic collapse
/ Peter Goodchild.

ISBN 978-1-55483-108-1 (pbk.)

1. Survival. 2. Subsistence farming. 3. Petroleum reserves--
Forecasting. I. Title.

GF86.G65 2013   613.6'9   C2013-906510-5

The publisher gratefully acknowledges the support of the Department of Canadian
Heritage through the Canada Book Fund.

Printed and bound in Canada

Insomniac Press
520 Princess Avenue, London, Ontario, Canada, N6B 2B8
www.insomniacpress.com

For Kerstin

Contents

Foreword

William R. Catton, Jr., Professor Emeritus
Washington State University

Human inhabitants of planet Earth have cleverly devised ways to progress and prosper by using ever more of Earth's substance, in ever more intricate ways. This cleverness has created a serious predicament. As I try to follow Peter Goodchild's example by attempting to think post-peak-oil, post-peak-iron-ore, post-peak-H_2O, post-peak-arable-land, and post-depletion-of-many-other-necessities, a popular line from the musical *Fiddler on the Roof* hauntingly intrudes, focusing my reaction to this courageous analysis of our predicament. Putting aside the melody and embracing the drama's simple words: "I wish I were a rich man . . ." I find myself pinpointing that wish: ". . . so I could afford to *give away* at least 535 copies of *Tumbling Tide*." If every member of the US Senate and every member of the House of Representatives were simultaneously to receive donated copies and be urged to read them, how might this change their conversations with one another, and their subsequent legislating actions?

Were there some moneyed philanthropist awaiting just such an opportunity, he or she might also choose to donate copies to leaders of the world's various organized religions. Too many religious leaders have been as stubbornly pro-natalist as politicians, naïvely committed to the notion that this planet, fundamentally finite, can always accommodate an ever-growing load of resource using inhabitants, many with expanding resource appetites. Perhaps our hypothetical philanthropist would pray that enough such recipients of this treatise, who customarily suppose themselves providers of moral and practical guidance for navigating global society into the future, would not merely read, but actually comprehend, absorb, and act upon Goodchild's perceptive interpretation of civilization's history. Would they respond to his detailed elucidation of the sad nature of today's human prospect and its fundamental cause?

Everyone needs to see how we humans did entrap ourselves by our vaunted progress. We have equated growth, both in numbers and in material output, with progress. Yet continued growth on a finite planet leads eventually to per capita scarcity of resources. Even the basis for survival diminishes as growth leads to excess.

Peter Goodchild has clearly recognized all this and dared to advocate the drastic change of course so urgently needed now. But given the deeply ingrained predilections of so-called *Homo sapiens*, the required course correction is terribly improbable. Without the necessary and drastic redirection, the not-so-wise experiment that the existence of our species has represented, remains headed for immanent termination.

Collapse of global civilization will come, not just from evil machinations by villains but from the circumstances all of us, innocently and hopefully, have helped create, have generally supported, and upon which we have become dependent. Collapse, especially if misunderstood, is likely to entail prodigious suffering, as we seek culprits against whom to "retaliate" for our mounting misfortunes!

We humans must promptly wise up, outgrow hubris, learn humility and compassion, and decide to use our planetary habitat with severe modesty. Or else . . .

William R. Catton, Jr. is the author of *Overshoot: The Ecological Basis of Revolutionary Change* and *Bottleneck: Humanity's Impending Impasse.*

Preface

The following pages sometimes have more to do with meditation than with measurement; the days to come are not easy to quantify. The focus is roughly on the year 2010, since that is a close-enough approximation to the year of "peak oil," although that date still has a few uncertainties. The future, however, is sometimes a matter of crystal gazing or, at best, of comparative studies. Basically the topic involves consideration of hypotheses and thought experiments, although human behaviour on a large scale has so many variables that it is at times on no higher level of predictability than the weather.

To some extent, the complexities in the story can be reduced by focusing on Americans, not as villains but as a group of people who are typical of modern industrial society, who have great influence, and about whom there is considerable information. To be even more precise in my terms and definitions, and in view of the similarities, I should add my own country and say "Americans and Canadians," but that would be a cumbersome term.

The focus is also on what might be called cultural issues, or perhaps even spiritual ones, although the latter term is not meant in any particularly religious sense. Not that explaining one's "position," compared to anyone else's, is of any great importance: the future will do whatever it wants to do, no matter how much it is analyzed or by whom. Nevertheless, I hope my initial prejudices and presumptions are obvious enough to explain a few odd twists in the path of the tale.

Those who see the coming centuries as significantly different from the present are sometimes accused of preaching gloom and misery, but it might be argued that instead of dwelling on peripheral details of science or economics, one might start thinking about practical ways of dealing with the future. Perhaps that concern for practicality is a good reason for choosing the title of "survivalist," even if others use the word in a disparaging sense. Surely, however, being a survivalist is better than trying to conjure up proofs that the problems do not exist.

I suspect that ultimately a return to the old ways of living, if such is the case, would not be so unfortunate. Human beings were foragers and farmers for a very long time, and they seem to have done well enough. They lived in a less crowded world; for them the land, the sea, and the sky were still beautiful. Perhaps there will come a day when, like our early ancestors, we can move at a slower pace, watching the forest, or the waves of the ocean, or fields of grain rippling under a summer wind.

1
Oman in Winter

Tourist brochures of Oman give the impression of a country leaping into the modern era, as if the Arabia of T. E. Lawrence were being transformed now, not by biplanes but by Toyotas. But what I see is the reverse: that Oman, on the edge of the world's largest oil fields, is not a "developing" country, but rather a declining one. Even making allowances for the fact that sloth is a sign of nobility, what is obvious is the pervasive inefficiency.

Oman is said to have oil reserves of about 5 billion barrels, although recoverable reserves may be more like 3 billion. In a world that uses 30 billion barrels a year, a grand total of 3 billion is not much. What will happen when that oil is gone?

And what will happen when the water is gone? I sometimes walk from my apartment on the north end of town to a deserted village of clay-brick houses. On my first visit I come upon two huge wells from which the villagers once drew their water. They are neatly built, with four straight walls, but there is not a drop of water in them. There are also several *aflaj*, irrigation channels, running through that village from some place in the nearby mountains where the water table is higher. There is no water in the *aflaj*, and this is December, the month when there is an occasional drop of rain. If there is no water in December, there will be none all year.

There are many such villages now deserted, because they have been replaced by buildings of concrete block, ugly structures with the acoustics of cells on death row. There are not many working *aflaj* of the traditional sort now, although they were once the pride of Oman, because the water table has dropped too far. Now the buildings in my part of town are supplied by water trucks, with heavy motors hammering the water into the apartments.

The big plan, however, is to replace all the older systems of water delivery with oil-fired desalination plants. The pipes lie beside the highway, ready to be connected and buried. Desalination plants have a reputation for malfunctioning. A larger question, however, is: What will happen to these plants when the fossil fuels to run them have disappeared?

The population of Oman is six times larger than in 1950. Over 95 percent of the country is classified as hyper-arid. Out of 160 countries analyzed by the Food and Agriculture Organization of the United Nations in terms of potential for future agricultural growth, Oman is the absolute last in rank (Bot, Nachtergaele, & Young, 2000). This country must therefore be added to the long lists in Kaplan's *Ends of the Earth* (2001), a grim look at decaying societies throughout the world. The twenty-first century has been badly pasted onto the seventh.

Out at one of the schools, observing the progress of Omani students I'm training to be English teachers, I hear an Arabic version of "Old MacDonald Had a Farm," and I think about the long airplane flight that brought me so far from home, to such a strange land. In general the Omani, at least the young, are a people of physical grace and beauty, and half of my nervousness may be merely that of the physically decadent among a race of warriors. The plumbing in my apartment is merely a collection of pipes that barely hangs onto the walls. Those who have the ability to repair anything have their chins in the air because a sheik does no labour. I pay more than I should for everything, since the gracious host who is supposed to be helping us foreigners always takes a kickback. The extremely high death rate on the highways seems to bother nobody but myself. I watch cars nosedive into each other in front of my own vehicle, another of the brand-new white Toyotas. Patience, patience, as they say on death row. I mustn't take everything so seriously. "When the oil runs out," says one of my students, "we'll return to the traditional ways. We'll go back to riding donkeys."

2
Elements of Collapse

Systemic collapse, the coming dark age, the coming crash, overshoot, the die-off, the tribulation, the coming anarchy, resource wars—there are many names, and they do not all correspond to exactly the same thing, but there is a widespread conviction that something ominous is happening. This event has about 10 elements, each with a somewhat causal relationship to the next. The first are (1) fossil fuels, (2) metals, and (3) electricity. These are a tightly knit group, and no industrial civilization can have one without the others.

As those three disappear, (4) food becomes scarce—grain and fish supplies, for example, have been declining for years. (5) Fresh water also becomes scarce—water tables are falling everywhere, rivers are not reaching the sea. Matters of infrastructure then follow: (6) transportation and (7) communication—no paved roads, no telephones, no computers. After that, the social structure begins to fail. (8) Government (and the economy) is characterized by income disparity, kleptocracy, inflation, and artificial debt crises. (9) Education sinks to ever-lower levels. (10) Large-scale division of labour starts coming to an end, although it was largely that which made complex technology possible.

It should be mentioned that when discussing the 10 elements the terms *sustainable*, *overshoot*, and *carrying capacity* are usually not very helpful. In *Overshoot* (1982), William Catton discovered and discussed a great range of these concepts, but some of the more-recent attempts to define the terms lead into ambiguities and self-contradictions. As a result, they often serve merely as buzzwords and fail to clarify the basic issues.

After those 10 elements, there are others forming a separate layer. These are in some respects more psychological or sociological, and are far less easy to delineate, but we might refer to them as "the four Cs." The first three are (1) crime, (2) cults, and (3) craziness—a world in which selfishness and deceit replace a sense of community; the ascendancy of dogmas based on superstition, ignorance, cruelty, and intolerance; the overall tendency toward anti-intellectualism; and the inability to distinguish mental health from mental illness.

Those three are followed by a final and more general element that is (4) chaos, which results in the pervasive sense that "nothing works anymore." Think of the future US as a transplant from one of the least-fortunate parts of the ex-Soviet world: drunken police officers in ill-fitting uniforms, parks strewn with garbage, and apartment buildings devoid of straight lines. Although difficult to identify, the subtle or even subliminal indications of general dysfunction become glaringly obvious.

3
Oil Production

Oil is everything. That is to say, everything in the modern world is dependent on oil and other hydrocarbons. From these we get fuel, fertilizer, pesticides, lubricants, plastic, paint, synthetic fabrics, asphalt, pharmaceuticals, and many other things. On a more abstract level, we are dependent on these fossil fuels for manufacturing, for transportation, for agriculture, for mining, and for electricity. When oil goes, our entire industrial society will go with it. There will be no means of supporting the billions of people who now live on this planet. Above all, there will be insufficient food.

A good deal of debate has gone on about that "peak," the date at which the world's annual oil production will reach (or did reach) its maximum and will begin (or did begin) to decline. (Of course, it is actually extraction; we do not "produce" oil, just as dentists do not "produce" teeth.) The exact numbers are unobtainable, mainly because individual countries give rather inexact figures on their remaining supplies. The situation can perhaps be summarized by saying that dozens of major studies have been done, and the consensus is that the peak is somewhere between the years 2000 and 2020. Within that period, a middle date seems rather more likely. Some of the data are discussed in more detail in the Appendices.

After the "peak" itself, the next question is that of the annual rate of decline. Estimates tend to hover around 3 or 4 percent, which means production will fall to half of peak production at some time around 2030, although there are reasons to suspect the decline will be much faster, particularly if Saudi reserves are seriously over-stated (Simmons, 2006).

In 1850, before commercial production began, there may have been 2 trillion barrels of usable, recoverable oil in the ground. By about the year 2010, roughly half of that oil had been consumed, but perhaps as much as 1 trillion barrels remain. A trillion may sound like a great deal, but is not really so impressive in terms of how long it will last. At the moment, about 30 billion barrels of oil are produced annually, and that is probably close to the maximum that will ever be possible. When newspapers announce the discovery of a deposit of a billion barrels, readers are no doubt amazed, but they are not told that such a find is only two weeks' supply. Many press re-leases, particularly about "unconventional oil," are just thinly disguised advertising, designed to lure gullible in-vestors into supporting projects that will have large ex-penses but small profits.

Coal and natural gas are also not as plentiful as be-fore. Coal will be available for a while after oil is gone, although previous reports of its abundance were highly exaggerated. Coal, however, is highly polluting and can-not be used as a fuel for most forms of transportation. In addition, coal mining requires large amounts of oil (mostly in the form of diesel fuel) and electricity. As for natural gas, it is not easily transported, it is not suitable for most equipment, and again it is a fossil fuel less abundant than often claimed to be, even with hydraulic fracturing of shale.

In terms of its effects on daily human life, the most significant aspect of fossil fuel depletion will be the lack of food. "Peak oil" basically means "peak food." Modern agriculture is highly dependent on fossil fuels for fertilizers (the Haber-Bosch process combines natural gas with atmospheric nitrogen to produce nitrogen fertilizer), pesticides, and the operation of machines for irrigation, harvesting, processing, and transportation. Without fossil fuels, modern methods of food production will disappear, and crop yields will be far less than at present. We should therefore have no illusions that 7 billion humans can be fed by "organic gardening" or anything else of that nature.

Much of modern warfare is about oil, in spite of all the rhetoric about the forces of good and the forces of evil (Klare, 2002). The real "forces" are those trying to control the oil wells and the fragile pipelines that carry that oil. A map of American military ventures over the last few decades is a map of petroleum deposits.

The ascent and descent of oil production were discovered long ago. Studying American oil fields in the 1950s, a geoscientist at Shell named M. King Hubbert found that as the years went by, oil production decreased, mainly because big discoveries were becoming less common, while new discoveries were becoming fewer and smaller. The changes in production could be plotted on a graph, forming something resembling a bell curve (Grove, 1974, June; Hubbert, 1956). Looking at the graph, Hubbert could see that the peak of American oil production would be about 1970; after that, there would be a permanent decline. When he announced this, most people laughed at him. But he was right: after 1970, American oil production went into a decline from which it never recovered.

Hubbert also reasoned that the same sort of pattern must be true of oil production in the whole world, not just in the US. Plotting the available data, he calculated that global production would peak in 1995. His reasoning about the world situation was the same as that for the US: the big discoveries were lessening, and newer discoveries were becoming fewer and smaller. Again he was right, or at least he was nearly right: in 1960, about 7 billion barrels were being produced yearly, and in 2000 production had increased to nearly 30 billion, but the peak is close to the latter date.

4
Alternative Energy

Alternative sources of energy will never be very useful for several reasons, but mainly because of a problem of "net energy": the amount of energy output is not sufficiently greater than the amount of energy input (Gever, Kaufmann, & Skole, 1991). With the problematic exception of uranium, alternative sources ultimately don't have enough "bang" to replace the 30 billion barrels of oil we use annually—or even to replace more than the tiniest fraction of that amount.

At the same time, alternative forms of energy are so dependent on the very petroleum that they are intended to replace that the use of them is largely self-defeating and irrational. Petroleum is required to produce, process, and transport almost any other form of energy; a coal mine is not operated by coal-powered equipment. It takes "oil energy" to make "alternative energy." Alternative energy, in other words, is always riding on the back of a vast fossil-fuel civilization.

The use of unconventional oil (shale deposits, tar sands, heavy oil) poses several problems besides that of net energy. Large quantities of natural gas and water are needed to process the oil from these unconventional sources. The pollution problems are considerable, and it is not certain how much environmental damage the human race is willing to endure. With unconventional oil we are, almost literally, scraping the bottom of the barrel.

More exotic forms of alternative energy are plagued with even greater problems (Younquist, 2000, October). Fuel cells cannot be made practical because such devices require hydrogen obtained by the use of fossil fuels (coal or natural gas), if we exclude designs that will never escape the realm of science fiction; if fuel cells ever became popular, the fossil fuels they require would be consumed even faster than they are now. Biomass energy (from corn or wood, for example) requires impossibly large amounts of land and still results in insufficient quantities of net energy, perhaps even negative quantities. Wind and geothermal power are only effective in certain areas and for certain purposes. Hydroelectric dams are reaching their practical limits. Nuclear power will soon be suffering from a lack of fuel and is already creating serious environmental dangers.

The current favourite for alternative energy is solar power, but it has no practicality on a large scale. There is a great deal of solar energy reaching the Earth, but it is too diffuse to be of much value. A good analogy to that diffusiveness, and in fact a somewhat related problem, is that metals have been of use to humankind only because they were found in concentrated deposits.

Proponents of solar energy must therefore close their eyes to all questions of scale. The world's deserts have an area of 36 million km², and the solar energy they receive annually is 300,000 exajoules (EJ), which at a typical 11 percent electrical-conversion rate would result in 33,000 EJ (Knies, 2006). Annual global energy consumption in 2005 was approximately 500 EJ. To meet the world's present energy needs by using thermal solar power, then, we would need an array (or an equivalent number of smaller ones) with a size of 500/33,000 x 36 million km^2, which is about 550,000 km^2—a machine the size of France. The production and maintenance of this array would require vast quantities of hydrocarbons, metals, and other materials—a self-defeating process. Solar power will therefore do little to solve the world's energy problems.

The quest for alternative sources of energy is not merely illusory; it is actually harmful. By daydreaming of a noiseless and odourless utopia of windmills and solar panels, we are reducing the effectiveness of whatever serious information is now being published. When news articles claim that there are simple painless solutions to the oil crisis, the reader's response is not awareness but drowsiness. We are rapidly heading toward the greatest disaster in history, but we are indulging in escapist fantasies. All talk of alternative energy is just a way of evading the real issue: that the Industrial Age is over.

Petroleum, unfortunately, is the perfect fuel, and nothing else even comes close. The problem with the various flying pigs of alternative energy (as in "when pigs can fly") is not that we have to wait for scientists to perfect the technology; the problem is that the pig idea is not a good one in the first place. To maintain an industrial civilization, it's either oil or nothing.

5
Infrastructure

Most schemes for a post-oil technology are based on the misconception that there will be an infrastructure, similar to that of the present day, which could support such future gadgetry. Modern equipment, however, is dependent on specific methods of manufacture, transportation, maintenance, and repair. In less abstract terms, this means machinery, motorized vehicles, and service depots or shops, all of which are generally run by fossil fuels. In addition, one unconsciously assumes the presence of electricity, which energizes the various communications devices, such as telephones and computers; electricity on such a large scale is only possible with fossil fuels.

To believe that a non-petroleum infrastructure is possible, one would have to imagine, for example, solar-powered machines creating equipment for the production and storage of electricity by means of solar energy. This equipment would then be loaded on to solar-powered trucks, driven to various locations, and installed with other solar-powered devices, and so on, ad absurdum and ad infinitum. Such a scenario might provide material for a work of science fiction, but not for genuine science—and, most certainly, not in the context of the next few years.

It is not only oil that will soon be gone. Iron ore of the sort that can be processed with primitive equipment is becoming scarce, and only the less-tractable forms will be available when the oil-powered machinery is no longer available. Copper and other metals are also in decline. These materials are now becoming irretrievably scattered among the world's garbage dumps.

The infrastructure will no longer be in place: oil, electricity, and asphalt roads, for example. Partly for that reason, the necessary social structure will also no longer be in place: efficient government, high-level education, and large-scale division of labour.

Without the infrastructure and the social structure, it will be impossible to produce the familiar goods of industrial society. Without fossil fuels, the most that is possible is a pre-industrial infrastructure, although one must still ignore the fact that the pre-industrial world did not fall from the sky in a prefabricated form but took countless generations of human ingenuity to develop. Furthermore, pre-industrial technology had a very much smaller population to support.

Fossil fuels, metals, and electricity are all intricately connected. Each is inaccessible on the modern scale without the other two. Any two will vanish without the third. If we imagine a world without fossil fuels, we must imagine a world without metals or electricity. What we imagine, at that point, is a society far more primitive than the one to which we are accustomed—and also far more primitive than the one our great-grandparents knew.

6
Farmland

With "low technology," i.e., technology that does not use fossil fuels, crop yields diminish considerably. David Pimentel explains that the production of so-called field or grain corn (maize) without irrigation or mechanized agriculture is only about 2,000 kilograms per hectare. That is less than a third of the yield that a farmer would get with modern machinery and chemical fertilizer (Pimentel, 1984; Pimentel & Hall, 1984; Pimentel & Pimentel, 2007).

Yields for corn provide a handy baseline for other studies of population and food supply. At the same time, corn is an ideal crop for study because of its superiority to others: it is one of the most useful grains for supporting human life. For the Native people of the Americas, it was an important crop for thousands of years (Weatherwax, 1954). Corn is high-yielding and needs little in the way of equipment, and the more ancient varieties are largely trouble-free in terms of diseases, pests, and soil depletion. If it can't be done with corn, it can't be done with anything. Of course, in reality no one would live entirely on corn; the figures here serve merely as a basis of comparison with other crops in a mixed diet.

A hard-working (i.e., farming) adult burns about 1 million kilocalories ("calories") per year. The food energy from a hectare of corn grown with "low technology" is about 9 million kilocalories (Pimentel, 1984). Under primitive conditions, one hectare of corn would support only nine people. Those figures are rather idealistic, however. We are assuming that people will follow a largely vegetarian diet; if not, they will need much more land. We need to allow for fallow land, cover crops, and green manure, for inevitable inequities in distribution, and for other uses of the land. We must account for any rise in population. Finally, most other crops require more land than corn in order to produce the same yield. On a global scale, a slightly more realistic ratio would be four people to each hectare of arable land, and even a figure that high does not seem to be supported by the facts of daily life, i.e., the available evidence of poverty and overcrowding. Even then, we have not yet discussed the problem that agriculture is a fundamentally unsustainable activity: sooner or later, all land loses its original fertility.

The average American house lot is about a tenth of a hectare, including the land on which the house is sitting (Mason, 2010). Those who expect to get by with "victory gardens" are therefore unaware of the arithmetic involved. Perhaps some of that misunderstanding is due to the misconception that humans can live on "vegetables" in the narrow sense of the word, i.e., in the sense of "green vegetables" as opposed to grains, which are vegetables only in the sense that they are also members of the Vegetable Kingdom. In reality, it is not "vegetables" in the former sense but grains that are the present foundation of human diet.

During the Neolithic Era, our ancestors took various species of grass and converted them into the plants on which human life now depends. Wheat, rice, corn, barley, rye, oats, sorghum, millet: these are the grasses people eat every day. It is members of the grass family that are used in raising the pigs and cows that are killed as other food. A diet of green vegetables would be slow starvation; it is grains that supply the thousands of kilocalories that keep us alive from day to day. There are reasons to question the benefits of a diet of cultivated grains (Ferguson, 2003, July/August), but at least over the next few decades it will be the localized production of grains that will support those who survive the collapse of civilization.

In the entire world there are now about 15 million km^2 of arable land (Bot, Nachtergaele, & Young, 2000; CIA, 2010). This is about 10 percent of the world's total land area. The present world population is over 7 billion. Dividing the figure for population by that for arable land, we see that there are about 470 people per km^2 of arable land. On a smaller scale that means about five people per hectare, more than the above-mentioned ideal ratio of 4:1. In fact, most of the world's two hundred or so countries have more than seven people per hectare; these countries, in other words, are perhaps already beyond the limits of the number of people who can be supported by non-mechanized agriculture. The UK, for example, has a population-to-arable ratio of slightly more than ten people per hectare; what exactly is going to happen to the six people who will not fit onto the hectare? But many countries have far worse ratios.

7
Population

The world's population has risen from about 1.7 billion in 1900 to 2.5 in 1950, and is over 7 billion now. Most of this increase, of course, has been in "developing" countries, suggesting that the term *developing* is rather misleading: a combination of environmental degradation and rapid population growth often makes "development" impossible (Catton, 1982; Kaplan, 2001). It has been said that without fossil fuels the global population must drop to about 2 or 3 billion (Youngquist, 2000, October), although even a number of that size is questionable. In terms of agriculture alone we would not be able to accommodate the present number of people as fossil fuels become scarce with manual labour instead of automation, and without the hydrocarbon-based fertilizers and pesticides that make modern yields triple those of earlier times (Pimentel, 1984; Pimentel & Hall, 1984; Pimentel & Pimentel, 2007).

Even then we have not factored in war, epidemics, and other aspects of social breakdown. The above-mentioned figure of 2 or 3 billion as a surviving population may be wildly optimistic. In fact, if we assume that agriculture is ultimately unsustainable (Ferguson, 2003, July/August; Lee, 1968), we must regard a final global population of about 10 million, as existed 10,000 years ago, as more likely.

Overpopulation is the fundamental cause of systemic collapse (Catton, 1982). All of the flash-in-the-pan ideas that are presented as solutions to the modern dilemma—solar power, biofuels, hybrid cars, desalination, permaculture, enormous dams—have value only as desperate attempts to solve an underlying problem that has never been addressed in a more direct manner. American foreign aid has always included only trivial amounts for family planning (Spiedel et al., 2009, January); it would seem that the most powerful country in the world has done very little to solve the biggest problem in the world.

The problem of overpopulation is worsened by the fact that there are many people busy either transmitting or receiving disinformation about the subject (Kolankiewicz & Beck, 2001, April). For left-wingers, discussion of high population is seen as persecution of the world's poor. For right-wingers, high population is seen as providing more buyers, more workers, and more investors. For politicians, more people means more votes. For many religious groups, high population reflects God's command to go forth and multiply. Corporate funding of several major environmentalist groups has also done quite a job of disconnecting them from discussion of population: they may be "green," but they are no longer "clean."

Overpopulation can always be passed off as somebody else's problem. It is the fundamental case of what Garrett Hardin calls "the tragedy of the commons" (1968, 1995): although an oversize family may have a vague suspicion that the world will suffer slightly from that fecundity, no family wants to lose out by being the first to back down. Without a central governing body that is both strong and honest, however, the evasion is perpetual, and it is that very lack of strength and honesty that makes traditional democracy an anachronism to some extent.

The Chinese have made quite an effort at dealing with excess population growth, but even they have not been entirely successful. Since 1953, the year of the first proper Chinese census and approximately the start of concerns with excessive fertility, the population has gone from 583 million to over 1.3 billion. For that matter, since the official starting of the one-child campaign in 1979, the population has grown by over 300 million (Riley, 2004, June); in other words, China's increase is equal to the entire population of the US.

Overpopulation, however, is a problem that occurs not only in poor countries. The evidence is also clear in the US:

Mounting traffic congestion; endless disruptive road construction; spreading smog; worsening water pollution and tightening water supplies; disappearing wildlife habitats, farmland, and open spaces; overcrowded schools; overused parks and outdoor recreation facilities; the end of small-town life in communities that until recently had been beyond the city; the impending merging together of separate, unwieldy metropolitan areas into vast megalopolitan miasmas; and the overall deterioration in quality of life and the increasing social tensions of urban dwellers reflected in such phenomena as gated communities and road rage (Kolankiewicz & Beck, 2001, April).

It is only in the hinterlands, away from the cities, that the opposite occurs: depopulation and "rural flight." The causes of depopulation are many, but they begin with the industrialization of agriculture and the growth of enormous corporate farms, "agribusiness." As the farming population is impoverished and reduced, the peripheral economy also shrinks, and crime and other social problems are the result. Nevertheless, the urban population of a country increasingly outweighs the rural. Worldwide, slightly more than half the human population now lives in urban areas, but these places will be death traps as resources disappear. For many, however, the choice between rural and urban will be difficult.

(Depopulation in the midst of overpopulation is a curious paradox, yet it exists. One might think the solution to rural poverty and the consequent depopulation would be some sort of "agrarian revival," the development of self-sufficient communities. But it just doesn't happen. People living in the country would rather drive many kilometres to a supermarket than support local agriculture. They will never get out of that mental world. Their parents grew up on farms, so they themselves want to be part of modern society, even if modern society came to an end several decades ago. They dream of getting the federal government to put up a skyscraper and give everyone desk jobs. It would be possible for an "agrarian revival" to succeed, but only if all the people in a community worked together. But that is the crux of the problem: there is only one thing rural families hate more than newcomers, and that's other rural families that have been living in that village for generations. Asians are collectivists; Caucasian westerners are individualists, and that will contribute to their downfall.)

Actually, "overpopulation" tends to be a euphemism for "overimmigration." Every country in the world is already well populated, in most cases quite overpopulated. The conception of some sort of land that is lying empty, waiting for the blessing of new arrivals, is a fiction invented by dishonest politicians. Family planning organizations sometimes inadvertently help to propagate this myth by euphemism, excessive caution in phraseology, and an unwillingness to risk antagonism. Although "family planning" is an admirable goal, what such organizations rarely state is that it is not where a child is born that really matters, demographically and economically, but where that person is eventually living—not the moment of birth, but the decades between birth and death, during which time that person will be consuming the world's resources, along with 7 billion other people doing the same. Emigration and immigration, transferring the problem of overcrowding from one country to another, do no good at all; if anything, they simply perpetuate the illusion that birth control is unnecessary.

Discussion of overpopulation, however, is a great taboo. Politicians will rarely touch the issue. Many documents from the United Nations merely sidestep the issue by discussing how to cater to large populations, in spite of the fact that such catering is part of the problem, not part of the solution.

To speak against overpopulation is an exercise in futility. How likely is it that the required massive change in human thinking will ever take place? Even in "developed" countries, to broach the topic of overpopulation is often to invite charges of racism and elitism. And there seems something both naïve and presumptuous in the common liberal American belief that people in poor countries are waiting to be enlightened to American ideals. On the contrary, the inhabitants of poor countries are often quite determined to hang on to their present systems of politics and religion, no matter how archaic and oppressive those systems may seem to outsiders, and would prefer that any proselytizing go in the opposite direction. Indeed, there is the frightful possibility that one reason why the US government gives so little aid to some countries is that the problem of overpopulation is regarded as hopeless, and any assistance would be just money down the drain (Kaplan, 2001). Instead of dreaming of ways to reduce a population of several billion to a reasonable number overnight, therefore, it might be more sensible to think in terms of the medical system of triage: let us save those who can be saved.

Like so many other species, humanity expands and consumes until its members starve and die. The basic problem of human life, the imbalance of population and resources, has still never been solved. As a result, the competition for survival is intense, and for most people life is just a long stretch of drudgery followed by an ignoble death. It is ironic that birth control, the most important invention in all of human history, has been put into practice in such a desultory manner. Why are we looking for intelligent life on other planets when there is still so little of it on Earth?

In view of the general unpopularity of birth-control policies, it can only be said euphemistically that Nature will decide the outcome. It is St John's Four Horsemen of war, famine, plague, and death who will signify the future of the industrial world. Nor can we expect people to be overly concerned about good manners. Although there are too many variables for civil strife to be entirely predictable, if we look at accounts of large-scale disasters of the past, ranging from the financial to the meteorological, we can see that there is a point at which the looting and lynching begin. In fact, the basic cause of warfare throughout history and prehistory has been, quite simply, overpopulation and the subsequent lack of food (Harris, 1989). The survivors of industrial society will have to distance themselves from the carnage.

The need for a successful community to be isolated from the rest of humanity is also a matter of access to the remaining natural resources. With primitive technology, it takes a great deal of land to support human life. What may look like a long stretch of empty wilderness is certainly not empty to the people who are out there picking blueberries or catching fish. That emptiness is not a prerogative or luxury of the summer vacationer. It is an essential ratio of the human world to the non-human: several square kilometres per family.

8
The End of Electricity

The first distinct sign of systemic collapse will be the increasing frequency of electrical power failures (Duncan, 2000, November 13; 2005–06, Winter). Throughout the world, electricity comes mainly from coal, natural gas, nuclear power plants, or hydroelectric dams, and all of them are bad choices. Most electricity in the US and Canada is produced by fossil fuels, and in the US that generally means coal. The first problems with electricity will serve as an advance warning, but the greatest danger will occur years later as the production of fossil fuels and metals is itself reduced by the lack of electrical power.

The US and Canadian grid is a hopelessly elaborate machine—the largest machine in history—and it is perpetually operating at maximum load, chronically in need of better maintenance and expensive upgrading. Every part of these two countries will be in some danger of outage over the next few years, due to inadequate supplies of electricity (NERC, 2008). Texas may be in the greatest danger, whereas Quebec (with the advantage of hydroelectric dams) may be the safest area. But most Americans and Canadians still cannot think of a failure of electricity as anything more than a momentary side effect of a summer storm. In other parts of the world, the future is already here: the lights fade out daily after four or five hours, if they come on at all. Actually Americans and Canadians are in far better shape than the citizens of other countries. Thanks to political bungling, even "civilized" Britain will apparently be losing 40 percent of its electrical power in the next few years, because aging power stations—coal, oil, and nuclear—are being forced to close, but the years of planning required to build new ones have been overlooked (Booker, 2008, June 10; Harrabin, 2009, September 11).

The use of electricity worldwide rose 54 percent from 1990 to 2005, while the production of energy (for electricity and many other things) rose only 34 percent (BP, annual; Duncan, 2000, November 13; Duncan, 2005–06, Winter; EIA, 2008, December 31), so it will not always be possible to meet the demand for electricity. The result will be widespread power shortages, some of these deliberately imposed, some of them not.

It is easy to assume that the only issue with fossil-fuel depletion is the problem of what to put in our automobiles. But the effect of that depletion on the production of electricity will be a problem of at least equal seriousness. If we have unavoidable worldwide blackouts and brownouts, the final result will be a sudden and catastrophic chain reaction. Fossil fuels and electricity are tightly integrated. We cannot have one without the other. Without fossil fuels, we can produce little or no electricity. Conversely, without electricity, we lack the "nervous system" (a useful analogy, since nerves work by ion transfer) to control any equipment that uses fossil fuels.

The problem of electricity, therefore, is one more factor to be tossed into the synergistic muddle of fossil-fuel depletion. Perhaps what we should be thinking of is not the familiar slope of depletion depicted in most studies, but a figure consisting of a relatively gentle slope that continues for only a few more years and then becomes a steeper curve downward, as resource depletion enters what may be called a second phase, perhaps roughly simultaneous with an economic second phase signified by the disappearance of government and currency. When fossil fuels are inadequate for maintaining electricity, the further results will be manifold. Fossil-fuel production itself will cease, and so will a great deal else.

It is not only fossil fuels and electricity that form a tightly integrated group, but a triad: fuels, electricity, and metals. Without fossil fuels and electricity, we cannot produce metals. For now let us focus on the first two of the three, but we should never forget that the production of metals is also a vital issue.

When we no longer have enough energy to channel into necessary electricity production, the game is over. Yes, we can divert some energy sources away from other uses towards the production of electricity, but such a diversion causes its own problems. For better or worse, the sources of electricity are mainly hydrocarbons and will continue to be so for the foreseeable future. As these hydrocarbons reach the downslopes of their production curves, electricity will follow a fairly similar curve.

The only remaining question is how quickly the various events will unfold. That in turn must be subdivided into questions on such matters as the supplies of the sources (oil, natural gas, coal, hydroelectricity, nuclear power, etc.), on global production of goods and services, on global population, on the amount of electricity generation, and on the chances of deliberately conserving electrical power.

We must not forget the above-mentioned chain reaction—the feedback mechanism. As less fuel (or any other source of energy) is available to produce electricity, there is less electricity to produce fuel. As less electricity is available to produce fuel, there is less fuel to produce electricity. The end is swift.

The answers are also complicated by the fact that the global data are not always reflected in more localized data. For some countries, blackouts and brownouts have been a way of life for years. But no country should assume that it is safe. In the US, the main energy source for electricity is coal, and there have been several reports that coal in the US is not as abundant as once assumed (Höök & Aleklett, 2009, May 1; Smith, 2009, June 8). The remaining coal is of poor quality and difficult to extract.

Richard C. Duncan emphasizes the fragility of electricity in the several versions of his "Olduvai essay." An important addition to his 2005–06 version is his emphasis on "proximate" versus "ultimate" causes of systemic collapse. "Permanent blackouts . . . will be the *proximate (direct, immediate)* cause of the collapse of industrial civilization. In contrast, [there will be] many *ultimate (indirect, delayed)* causes" (2005–06, Winter, p. 9; emphasis in the original).

Duncan also points out that the importance of electricity is overlooked because it is not the underlying giant problem of the limits to growth. As any science-minded person knows, electricity is not even a source of energy, it is merely a carrier of energy. Fossil fuels are the primary sources of energy in our industrial civilization. Yet electricity is subtle, and its importance is easily underestimated. It is *end use* that is significant:

> Electricity wins hands down as our most important end-use energy. To wit: I estimate that 7% of the world's oil is consumed by the electric power sector, 20% of the world's natural gas, 88% of the coal, and 100% each for nuclear and hydroelectric power. The result is that electric power accounts for 43% of the world's end-use energy compared to oil's 35% (Duncan, 2005–06, Winter, p. 4).

There are always many problems with the use of electricity. It is certainly costly. Duncan notes that, according to the International Energy Agency, the worldwide investment funds required for electricity from 2003 to 2030 will be about $9.66 trillion (2005–06). That sort of money is simply not available. Duncan also mentions that electric power systems are "complex, voracious of fuel, polluting, and require 24h-7d-52w maintenance and operations" (2000, November 13, p. 2).

Personally, I think of the great blackout of August 14, 2003, when a large part of northeastern North America came to a halt. Congress later called for up to $100 billion to renovate the power grid, but the money was spent on wars instead (Leopold, 2006, October 17). I remember that day very well. No gasoline, because the pumps required electricity. Still, many Torontonians came up to cottage country, where I was living, to wait out the troubles. There were no bank machines working, so it was cash only. There were big sales of batteries and candles, and of bottled water.

But that was only one day, with a few serious problems on following days. Independent generators kept hospitals and restaurants going. Water trucks solved a problem for cities that did not have gravity-fed reservoirs. But what if the problems had continued for a much longer time—perhaps forever—so that those clumsy attempts at rectification were no longer operating?

9
When the Lights Go Out

When the lights go out, so does everything else. There will come a time when the house or apartment will be largely non-functioning. Not only will there be darkness throughout the dwelling between sunset and sunrise, but all the sockets in the wall will be useless. The four major appliances—stove, refrigerator, washer, and dryer—will be nothing more than large white objects taking up space. There will be no familiar means of cooking food or preserving it, and no practical means of doing laundry. There will be no heating or air conditioning, because these are either controlled by electricity or entirely powered by it. For the same reason, the plumbing will not be working, so clean water will not be coming into the house, and waste water will not be leaving it. For those living in high-rise apartments, there will be many stairs to climb because the elevators will not be operational.

And that is only one's own habitation. The entire country will be affected; the whole world will be affected. Computers will cease to operate, and computers have insinuated themselves into almost every device we use. There will be no long-distance communication: no telephones, no Internet, no electronic transmission of data from anywhere to anywhere.

Eventually money will largely cease to exist, because there will be no electronic means of sending or receiving it, and no way of balancing accounts. Banking machines will cease to operate. In fact, money nowadays is generally not reckoned as coins or bills, but as data on a screen, and the data will no longer be there.

Modern medicine will vanish. Doctors will not have the modern means of taking care of their patients. Pharmacies will be closed, so drugs will not be available. Medicare will not be depositing funds into doctors' bank accounts. Hospitals will be burdened with the sick and dying, and there will be no means of taking care of the sick. With refrigeration not working, hospitals will not even be able to take care of the dead. There will not even be a means of removing and burying the bodies.

The police will be immobilized because they will have no means of sending or receiving information. Since police forces anywhere have only enough personnel to deal with fairly average crises (but not enough to deal with the great majority of minor crimes), their duties will be limited to protecting the rich and powerful. Eventually they will find that they are powerless to do anything but stay home and protect their own families.

There is a dangerous relationship between electricity and nuclear power. Nuclear reactors need electricity to run the cooling, among other things. As we have seen in several failures over the past few decades, a good-sized blackout could result in large-scale mortality from leaked radiation. The dangers are exacerbated by a combination of poor planning, poor regulation, and poor oversight, due to various fundamental human errors ranging from irresponsible cost-saving to outright fraud. Even the permanent closure of nuclear reactors, well ahead of time, will be hampered by a lack of both money and motivation—with so many people involved, it will be easy for everyone to shift responsibility to someone else.

It will be impossible to jump into a car and get help because cars require gasoline, and the gas pumps are run by electricity. In any case, the oil wells and the refineries will have ceased operation. The biggest "vicious circle" will have taken place: no electricity will mean no fossil fuels, and no fossil fuels will mean no electricity.

"When the lights go out" is largely a figure of speech, of course, because the incandescent or fluorescent light bulbs in a house will not be the major concern. In the daylight hours, one does not need light bulbs. But the flickering of bulbs will nevertheless act as an early-warning system—the canary in the coal mine, so to speak. During a severe storm, it is the flickering of light bulbs that indicates that it is time to get to whatever emergency supplies have been put aside: bottled water, canned food, and warm clothing. The unsolved problem, however, is that when most people think about emergencies, they only think about surviving and remaining comfortable for a short period of time. There is always the spoken or silent refrain of "until the authorities arrive." But those authorities will be waiting for other authorities to arrive, and those at the top will have made their own plans long ago.

Nevertheless, it must be said that there is a great deal that can be done. Of all the resources one can accumulate, the most important are those that are stored inside one's own head: knowledge, skills, and wisdom. *Knowledge* is perhaps not the right word, though, because to have read or heard about a particular fact does not automatically grant the ability to deal with particular issues.

Even more important than mere knowledge is practice. For example, I used to read a great many books on vegetable gardening, but when I owned and ran a market garden for several years I would occasionally mumble, "Why isn't this information in the books?" And there were several answers to that question. In the first place, most of the books were badly written; I consider the *Encyclopedia of Organic Gardening* (Bradley & Ellis, 1992) a major exception, even though my own gardening hardly counts as organic. Secondly, it is not the overall principles that count, but the minutiae. Thirdly, those particulars often cannot be put into writing or even into speech: "I can't explain it, I can only show you" is an expression I sometimes heard. A good gardener knows a thousand tiny tricks that lead to success, and it is those particulars that matter, not the general statement that one does not sprinkle seed in a snowstorm. (Actually the "simple life" takes a lifetime to learn, and one should really have the guidance of the previous generation.)

The skills needed for country living are rarely the same as those needed in the city, although anyone who has built up experience in such topics as home repair and improvement will be ahead of those whose knowledge consists of more ethereal matters. Hunting and fishing are not taught in academia.

When I say, "When the lights go out, so does everything else," I mean "everything in the city." What matters is not to be in the wrong place at the wrong time. Living in the city will most certainly be a case of the wrong place at the wrong time. There will be no food and no water, and no means of dealing with the victims of famine and disease. When there is an inkling that the electrical power everywhere is about to fail, the answer is to be well outside the city limits. One should either be living in the country or at least have some property in the country and a well-tested means of getting there.

Even a plan of that sort involves a few caveats. Property in the modern world is nothing more than a convenient legal fiction. If a gang of outlaws moves in next door, or even if there is a single oppressive neighbour to be dealt with, then the whole concept of "property" can vanish into thin air. I have known several cases in which people gave up house and land because they could not deal with troublemakers. What will it be like when the troublemakers are doing something more unpleasant than a little trespassing? So it is good to own property, but it is better to realize that ownership, in the modern sense of the word, might be nothing more than a scrap of paper.

Getting out of the city means knowing the roads— not the main highways, but the back roads. Cars will be less common in the future, but it is worth remembering that in a sudden emergency the main roads could become jammed, partly because of the volume of traffic but also because of accidents. Vehicles might even be abandoned, either because they are out of gas or because the passengers have discovered that it is quicker to walk. Knowing the back roads, and even knowing alternative routes among those back roads, means freedom of choice in one's movements.

The last matter is that of community. As mentioned above, the concept of property can be illusive, but there is more to consider in the question of who lives in the general area. Neighbours who take pleasure in noisy dogs, loud radios, or heavy drinking can make proximity unpleasant nowadays, but such people may not prevail in the kind of "natural selection" that will take place, where common decency will be everyone's concern. In any case, the greatest blessing of the post-petroleum age will be the demise of all-terrain vehicles, electronic amplifiers, and the other technological marvels with which people now ruin one another's enjoyment of "cottage country."

Even then, the trouble of having a neighbour may be less than the trouble of not having one. A family, a band, or a tribe makes it possible to distribute the various tasks that need to be done, whereas a loner might find it hard to cope. There are not many who have both the practical skills and the personality traits for complete independence; such people would have to be not only self-reliant but also live very far from any populated area if they are not to risk being outnumbered by evildoers.

It is not reasonable to expect a perfect neighbourhood. In the happiest primitive society there is gossip, discontent, jealousy, manipulation. Troubles and troublemakers can be dealt with in such a way that the community itself does not fall apart. In a primitive community, ostracism, for example, can be an effective means of resolving a problem. A community leader who lacks what we now call "managerial skills" can be replaced by one who does a better job. In any setting, neighbours are merely human, with common desires and antipathies and fears; it is important, not so much to wish for angelic neighbours, as to have enough daily contact with them to be able to anticipate how they will respond in a difficult situation.

10
The Pollyanna Principle

The problem of explaining peak oil does not hinge on the issue of peak oil as such, but rather on that of "alternative energy." Most people now have some idea of the concept of peak oil, but it tends to be brushed aside in conversation because of the common incantation: "It doesn't matter if oil runs out, because by then everything will be converted to [whatever] power." Humanity's faith in what might be called the Pollyanna Principle—the belief that everything will work out right in the end—is eternal.

The critical missing information in such a dialogue is that alternative energy will do little to solve the peak-oil problem, although very few people are aware of the fact. The Pollyanna Principle, after all, is what gets us through the day. Unfortunately, a quick glance through any standard textbook on world history would show that the principle does not apply to the many civilizations that lie buried in the mud. But to point at oil-production charts is to mistake a psychological problem for an engineering one; most people do not like to be pushed very far in the direction of the logical.

The main stumbling block, as noted above, is not the fact of the decline in world oil production, but the related fact of the impracticality of alternative energy.

Alternative sources of energy do have certain uses, and they always have had, especially in pre-industrial societies. However, it is not possible to use non-hydrocarbon sources of energy to produce the required amount of energy, and in a form that can be (1) stored conveniently, (2) pumped into cars, trucks, ships, and airplanes for the purpose of long-distance transportation of goods and people, (3) converted into a thousand everyday products, from asphalt to pharmaceuticals, and (4) used to run factories—and which costs so little that it can be purchased in large quantities on a daily basis by billions of people.

There is also the question of time. The entire conversion of world industry would have to be done virtually overnight. The peak of world oil production was probably around 2010. The more-important date of peak oil production per capita was 1979. There are approximately 1 billion automobiles and over 7 billion people. Throughout the twentieth century, food production only barely met global needs, and in the last few years it has not even reached that level. In terms of the amount of time available, the switch from hydrocarbon energy to an alternative form of energy would stretch the bounds of even the most fanciful work of science fiction.

But we don't even know the name of such an "alternative energy." Every month, the mainstream news media tell us of "the miracle of x power," but in the following month the x has been replaced by another provider of miracles. And even if that x were named, there would be the immense task of setting such a program in motion on a planetwide scale—half a century too late to do any good.

Contemplating the expense will also take us far into the realms of fantasy. At $10,000 (a fairly arbitrary figure, admittedly, but no real figures exist) per vehicle, replacing the vehicles that are now on the road would cost $10 trillion. The substructure—the ongoing manufacture, transportation, maintenance, and repair—would add much greater expense. The existing furnaces in all the world's buildings would be obsolete. Countless machines all over the planet would have to be replaced, countless factories redesigned. We would have to replace the asphalt on all the world's paved roads with a non-hydrocarbon substance. The money and resources simply do not exist. It is perhaps fortunate that there is no politician or business leader who would be willing to initiate such a mad venture.

In actuality, the world of the future will not be crowded. Survival for a few will be possible; survival for a population of billions will not be possible. But very few people have asked the ugly question of exactly how that rapid and dramatic reduction of population is going to take place. Voluntarily?

There are two further problems with trying to educate people on these matters. The first is that any discussion of either peak oil or alternative energy requires a scientific frame of mind: an understanding of empirical research and an ability to follow statistics without being misled. A grasp of basic science is essential in order to get a balanced perspective on the data and in order to judge between the practical and the impractical. The so-called civilized world is still largely the domain of astrology and other forms of superstition. Yet empirical research does not mean "I once saw something-or-other," and statistics are meaningless unless one understands exactly what is meant by "statistically significant."

The second of these further problems is that the concepts of peak oil and alternative energy are extremely complicated. Although it is possible to reduce those two topics to five hundred words or so, the problem with such a single-page explanation is that much of the vital information would be left out. If the document failed to mention every "and/but/or," the message would almost certainly be lost. If, on the other hand, the document were to be expanded to cover every minute particular, the writer would probably lose track of the average reader, since the text might exceed the latter's attention span.

The alternative energy problem can also be illuminated by an examination of similar dialogues on other topics, especially in cases where science clashes with its opposite. A discussion about creationism, for example, might entail hours of exhausting dialogue, to be terminated when the creationist party raises his head, takes a deep breath, and says, "Well, I believe . . . ." The conversation has reached a barrier, beyond which no travel is possible. When communication is in such a poor state, there is often little hope that a reader will go so far as to check citations, bibliographies, or further reading lists, or even to do something requiring as little labour as clicking on a hyperlink on a web page.

11
Post-Peak Economics

Almost everything in the global economy is either made from oil or requires oil to manufacture it or operate it. As the price of oil goes up, so does the price of everything else. This rise is referred to as "stagflation"—stagnant incomes combined with price inflation. The hardest hit will be those who have lost their jobs, followed by those with limited disposable income, which means those most likely to have debts: car payments, house mortgages, credit cards, student loans. But everyone will find that a dollar just doesn't stretch.

That will be Phase One: economic hardship. Besides stagflation, the major issues will be unemployment and a falling stock market. While money is still real, it will be everyone's obsession: as in Germany's Weimar Republic, it will take the proverbial wheelbarrow of money to buy a loaf of bread. The world of Phase One can be depicted as shoddy, dirty, and disorganized.

Phase Two, much longer, will be genuine chaos. It will be characterized by the disappearance of law and order and capable government. As these fade away, money will have no use as a medium of exchange. When there is no more faith in money, it will be replaced by barter. From economic hardship of a financial kind we will pass to economic hardship of a physical kind: manual labour and a scarcity of basic goods. The world of Phase Two will be a different picture, but at various times and for various people it will be shocking, horrifying, and deadly.

Phase One has already begun to some extent, to judge from three related events: (1) in 1970, US domestic oil production went into a permanent decline; (2) global oil production per capita reached its peak in 1979 (BP, annual); and (3) the price of oil roughly tripled from 2002 to 2012.

Phase Two can be envisioned by looking at events that unfolded when the Soviet Union collapsed in the 1990s. Within a short time, people simply gave up using money and switched to other items of exchange. One of the most common items was bottles of homemade vodka (Orlov, 2005). It seems that vodka was popular because it was easy to carry, of great practical value, and rather fixed in exchange value (since, presumably, it was either real vodka or it wasn't). But there are many cases similar to that of the Soviet Union. One might, for example, consider Argentina in 2001 (Aguirre, 2005, October 29). Or we might consider the American Civil War—after that time, Confederate dollars were literally just paper.

In other words, at one point the money problem will be everything, and a few decades later, the money problem will be nothing, because there won't be any money. Money is only a symbol, and it is only valuable as long as people are willing to accept that fiction: without government, without a stock market, and without a currency market, such a symbol cannot endure (Soros, 1998). Money itself will be useless and will finally be ignored. Tangible possessions and practical skills will become the real wealth. Having the right friends will also help.

It's important to remember the old clichés that money only exists as long as people have trust in it, whereas a currency that becomes suspicious simply dies. More specifically, money only exists as long as there is a government to produce the money and then to keep it alive. When a government utterly loses its power over the country, the money simply melts like snowflakes on a hot metal stove.

Will life be better or worse in a world without money? That's hard to say. When I lived for several years in a rural community in central Ontario, Canada, there seemed to be advantages to the rather casual and offhand bartering that went on. If one person left a gift on a neighbour's porch, and a few days later the neighbour left some other item on the first person's porch as a gesture of appreciation, it was not even clear if such behaviour could be considered barter.

There are parallels between the Great Depression of the 1930s and the present oil crash, but there are also important differences. The Great Depression was caused by overspeculation in the stock market, which led to the 1929 panic (Galbraith, 2009). The rapid sellout of stocks caused the collapse of many businesses. These businesses laid off many workers. The workers then had insufficient income to buy whatever was available, even though prices were low. The Great Depression, in other words, had an amazingly artificial cause, although the ensuing suffering was by no means artificial. The oil crash differs because its cause is not artificial; in fact, its cause has a rather uncertain relationship to the abstractions of economics. And although many people will lose their jobs, there will be no reduction in the prices of goods, at least in Phase One.

The Great Depression was a time of deflation. The basic cause was massive overspeculation, a great bubble that just burst. The problem today, on the other hand, is that our Commodity Number One, which is petroleum, is beginning to run out. That means that virtually all other commodities will likewise run out.

The era of the Great Depression, however, closely resembles the coming years in other respects. In particular, the poverty of that earlier time, and many other aspects of daily life, will be repeated in the events of future years— although that would be putting it mildly (Broadfoot, 1997).

In terms of the exigencies of daily life, part of the solution is to give up the use of money well ahead of time, instead of letting the money economy claim more victims. *Money economy* is not a tautology: materials and products were distributed or traded over very long distances long before money was invented; sometimes the process was simple barter, and at other times these matters were handled by a formal governing procedure. Barter would allow people to provide for their daily needs on a local basis, without the dubious assistance of governments or corporations. Such a way of doing business, unfortunately, is illegal if the participants are not paying sales tax on their transactions. Politicians disparage the age-old practice of barter as "the underground economy" or "the grey economy," but their own income is dependent on taxes. The transition itself would not be simple: there are so many rules, from building codes to insurance regulations to sales- and income-tax laws, that make it difficult to provide oneself with food, clothing, and shelter without spending money. Nevertheless, as the economy breaks down, so will the legal structure, and laws will become rather meaningless.

All that is certain about barter at the present time is that sales tax is not being paid, and that a "crime" is therefore being committed. The money economy requires that a large portion of one's income be paid out in various forms of legalized extortion: taxes, insurance, and banker's fees (such as mortgages), all of which are justified in our minds largely by the fact that they have been imposed for centuries.

Within the present economy there are also plain old bubbles, foolish speculation that causes some huge rises and falls in the prices of things. The most obvious one is housing. Another may be gold, although there are at least some plausible arguments for buying gold, beginning with the fact that it is a fairly hazard-free medium of exchange, at least in comparison with any form of currency.

Although inflation characterizes Phase One of economic collapse, inflation and deflation are never a case of either-or. The two can happen side by side, and usually have. Certainly today there are some things that are cheap, some things that are expensive.

The big inflationary items of today are food, oil, and gold. But they are not all the same case. Oil prices are rising because we are running out of oil. Food prices are also rising because we are running out of oil. In fact, anything is rising if it is connected to oil. Gold, however, is not directly connected to oil; it has value primarily as a preserver of wealth, even if that desire for wealth preservation is partly driven by oil fears.

Inflation, nevertheless, has to some extent been just a bogeyman in previous years (Greider, 1998). It was always the big financiers who did the most complaining about inflation because they were the ones who had the most to lose—their financial holdings thereby had less value in a fundamental sense. For the person who had no savings at all but whose wages were rising, inflation was really not a big issue. Nevertheless, in the twenty-first century inflation will matter, and very much so, at least until the big finale. The difference between the present and the past is that high prices are no longer connected to high wages.

We must certainly get rid of the old concept of inflationary-deflationary cycles. Toynbee and Spengler spoke of cycles of empires, but when we have all returned to living a simpler life, there will be cycles neither of inflation nor of empires.

The economic problem of peak oil is occurring when people in many countries have already gone through decades of being battered by other economic problems. One serious issue is globalization: for many years, big companies have been getting their work done by sending it out to whatever countries have the poorest people and the most repressive governments (Greider, 1998; Martin & Schumann, 1997; Thurow, 1996). The result is that people in the more-developed countries lose their jobs. Even when the official unemployment levels are low, the figures are misleading; large numbers of the employed are no longer working at well-paid, permanent jobs. Many are now working part-time, and others have given up hope of work. These factors are not counted in the official unemployment figures. Closely related to the problem of globalization is that of automation, which increases production but decreases payrolls. Economic disparity is therefore a characteristic of our times. For many years there has been a widening gap between the rich and the poor in the US: while most incomes have either fallen or not changed, the top 5 percent of families saw their incomes increase considerably (US Census Bureau, 2012).

As a result of all these vagaries within the capitalist system, government services are perpetually being cut. The common expression is that "money is tight these days," although very few people ask why that is the case. Taxes continue to rise, but the individual receives little in return. But the days of globalization and automation are coming to an end.

Ultimately, of course, all money is "funny money," because it is only a symbol of events occurring in the real world, and often it is a very inadequate symbol. For one thing, the rise and fall of oil prices often has little relation to how much is being produced, or how much is in the ground. What is more important is that the business world can multiply a symbol in order to create imaginary dollars, but the symbol then fails to reflect reality: such fictions as mortgage-backed securities, credit-default swaps, and collateralized debt obligations can make a few people rich but the majority of people considerably poorer. On a smaller scale, there is the question of what one dollar represents in the material world: if a "constant dollar" differs from a "current dollar," for example, then the word itself is so fluid that it is not really adequate as a measure of anything tangible. Whether the entirely artificial (anthropogenic) cataclysm of financial crises becomes more destructive than the partially "geological" cataclysm of natural-resource decline is hard to say, although the sheer artificiality of the former makes me doubtful.

There will certainly be some interactivity: if a sufficient number of people become impoverished, then the resulting demand destruction (a rather ponderous term referring to the loss in sales because of excessively high prices) will at least result in unsold petroleum and hence unfinanced oil exploration; beyond that the result may be that a combination of unpayable debt and unlimited money-printing will result in wholesale panic, and potatoes will replace money as a means of exchange.

12
Globalization

In the later decades of the twentieth century, partly because of computers and other forms of automation, there was a radical transformation of the world's economy: the human race became immersed in global capitalism. International companies were so big, so widespread, that they were free to make their own rules. The first principal effect of globalization was that companies could choose their workers from anywhere in the world. Conversely, those same companies could discard workers they did not want: the jobs went to the people who would accept the least pay, while most people in developed countries had to accept a lowering of their work status and a reduction in income.

The multinational corporations, the Fortune 500 companies, were making multi-billion-dollar profits, but they had also been joyfully downsizing for years, laying off many thousands of employees. Most Americans, in fact, had their incomes drop considerably after about 1980 (Thurow, 1996). The precise figure depends on which factors are selected: race, gender, age, employment status, and so on, but no matter how the analysis is applied, the figures still come out roughly the same. Income inequality, the gap between the rich and the poor, increased steadily over the years. The US was sliding back into the Victorian era, the world of Marx and Dickens.

The following years would include massive unemployment. It soon took many forms: the official figures were often misleading, and real jobs were increasingly replaced by less stable forms of employment. The official rate of unemployment in the US jumped considerably if one added the people who wanted jobs but were not officially part of the work force: the part-timers who would have liked to be full-timers; the people who were of the right age to be employed but who lived in an economic limbo, without visible means of support; those who worked "on call"; those who were day labourers or seasonal workers; those who tried to preserve their pride by calling themselves "independent contractors" or "consultants"; and those who were in the country with questionable political status (Thurow, 1996).

The problem of globalization began with the problem of automation, which created expansion and acceleration in three areas: production, communication, and transportation. Goods were built, ordered, and shipped with such efficiency that the other side of the world was just a step away. Automation had been hypnotizing humanity since the middle of the eighteenth century. It seemed a great blessing to be producing goods rapidly and at low cost. In 1811 the Luddites went around smashing machinery, in the belief that automation was depriving people of their jobs. Ever since then, the term *Luddite* was regarded as synonymous with "hopelessly old-fashioned person." As it turned out, the Luddites were right: the machines were of financial benefit to their owners, but not to the workers. In addition, the workers permanently lost their self-esteem because there were always too many people looking for jobs. In fact, the greater the degree of automation, the smaller the number of workers who were needed. Workers who protested, of course, were always the first to be fired and replaced.

As the twentieth century drew to a close, the true face of multinationalism could be seen. The shoes people wore on their feet were sold by a company that had its head office in a skyscraper in New York City, but the people who actually made the shoes were living in an impoverished country on the other side of the world. Those workers lived in a condition that was closer to true slavery than anything in North America (Greider, 1998; Martin & Schumann, 1997). The concepts of democracy and civil liberty were so unknown there that labour organizers could be imprisoned or killed.

International corporations always moved their factories to where they found the cheapest workers. A poor country thought it had hit the jackpot when a rich American corporation came to set up business. Unfortunately, if the factory started doing well, it was inevitable that the workers would start asking for slightly more than starvation wages, no matter how many activists were picked up at night to be tortured and killed by government-paid death squads. Even the government itself might start to become greedy. The workers might succeed, and the country's standard of living might rise. The punishment was simple: the international company packed up and moved to a country where the workers were still "uncorrupted." All this shopping for cheap wages—wage arbitrage—took jobs away from workers in the US and the rest of the developed world.

After Marx's time there was actually considerable progress in the reduction of working hours, thanks mainly to the relentless struggle by labour leaders and other "radicals" and "troublemakers." Slowly but surely, the average workweek of Americans dropped toward thirty hours, enabling both employment and wealth to be shared more equitably. Somewhat out of character, however, Roosevelt (later President) chose not to support the Black-Connery bill that would have put such a week into law; he later regretted his decision (Rifkin, 1995; Schor, 1991). But that was during the Great Depression, when most people were grateful for any kind of paying labour. After that came the Second World War, when it was one's patriotic duty to ask no questions. And not long after the war, Senator Joseph McCarthy was finishing off any radicals that might still be around. And then the workweek began to climb steadily upward.

We were creating a world in which a small minority of the population had money and power, and the rest were kept busy and kept out of mischief, but with neither money nor power (Martin & Schumann, 1997). Those who had grown crops for generations were losing their land as the corporate farm replaced the family farm. In the cities, young people were kept busy in colleges and universities, thinking they were on the road to success, but academic standards had fallen so low that a student loan was just a polite form of welfare payment.

Those who were kept busiest, most out of mischief, were an anachronistic group of people who had jobs but did not have either money or power: the truly "middle class," those in the median-income range. Both husband and wife had to work while the children were packed off to daycare centres. Household chores took up the evenings and weekends. A large part of their paycheques was bitten into by the mysterious national debt, and the rest was barely enough to cover the mortgage and groceries.

There was once a vision that automation would lead to a life of leisure and freedom. In 1930 J. M. Keynes was saying that "for the first time since his creation man will be faced with his real, his permanent problem—how to use his freedom from pressing economic cares, how to occupy the leisure, which science and compound interest have won for him, to live wisely and agreeably and well" (Keynes, 1952, p. 367). In 1969, the year of the first moon landing, it seemed as if computers would give us an age of tranquility and leisure, and that we would all be tiptoeing among the stars. If the Luddites were alive today, however, they would tell us that computers are devices for increasing production and decreasing payrolls. Automation proceeded with little regard for the benefit of the average person. If it was profitable to replace a worker with a clever electronic device, then it was done. But automation was only the hammer, not the hand that wielded it. The fundamental problem of globalization was that large corporations had become as powerful as entire countries.

13
A Smaller World

Historically democracy has often been combined with capitalism. Perhaps in the eighteenth century a combination of that sort seemed reasonable, but it has become far less so. Capitalism, by its very essence, means that each corporation is dedicated to its own success, no matter what the consequences may be for anyone else. Free enterprise is "healthy competition," yes, but only to a certain point.

The problem is that the big fish keep eating the smaller fish. When there is only one fish left, there is no more competition, healthy or otherwise. What is now in place, globally, is not free enterprise but thinly disguised monopolies or oligopolies. If there are only five or six corporations controlling an entire industry, and if those corporations indulge in frequent joint ventures, then it is absurd to be talking of free enterprise. And when monopolies cast their shadows over the land, the worker loses both economic and political freedom.

All political systems fall somewhere on the spectrum between absolute dictatorship and absolute democracy, i.e., between rule by one person and rule by all persons. Yet neither extreme has ever been met. No dictator has ever gone far without "legitimacy," without support from a fair number of his fellow citizens. Conversely, there has never been a perfect democracy, since Nature herself imposes too many inequalities for any system of justice to countervail.

Democracy certainly has its problems. From dawn to dusk, humans are obsessed with power, and such an obsession tends to preclude a system of "one person, one vote." In reality, it is "one dollar, one vote." Democracy also has a dozen other nemeses. For example, democracy (rule of the majority) frequently conflicts with another ideal, one with which it is inappropriately paired in idle rhetoric: individual liberty. My freedom to drive a car at top speed may conflict with society's wish that no one drive so quickly and thereby put people in danger.

At this stage in history, the biggest logistic problem with democracy is that most of the important issues are now beyond the understanding of the average person. In fact, the truly important economic events do not entail the production and distribution of goods, or even the production of services, but rather the movement of pure money, raw money. It is the daily shifting of large amounts of money, plain finance capital, that determines whether an individual person has a job tomorrow, and whether that same person can buy what he needs tomorrow.

To the old bromide that "democracy may not be the best form of government, but it's the best we have," I am inclined to reply, "Well, I'll wait for something better." Schoolchildren are told that ancient Greece was the founder of democracy, but neither Plato nor Aristotle had anything good to say about democratic government, even if those two differed on almost every other issue. When people lie in bed at night, they may dream of various social matters—peace, freedom, justice—but they do not dream of "democracy." The shift from one incumbent party to another makes little difference to the machinery of the civil service, and even less difference to the average person trying to pay for groceries and shelter. From one regime to the next is merely a matter of a few dollars more, a few dollars less, a little more lip service, a little less. People who put on their raincoats to "do their civic duty" by voting are, to a large extent, people who enjoy making fools of themselves.

The general corruption and dishonesty among politicians in modern democracies are so common that the topic can rarely even sell newspapers anymore. (But there is no reason to fear the loss of freedom of the press, since the press's few attempts at truth are largely ignored anyway.) The small voter turnout in any election is a sign of the anger and hopelessness that most people feel toward modern "democratic" government. What is wanted is a new life, a new birth, not the silliness of a false democracy.

The dangers of such a fraudulent political system are obvious. When the Nazis rose to power in the 1920s and '30s, it was not by ignoring "the will of the people" (to use Jefferson's words). On the contrary, Hitler's rise was sanctioned by both the government and the populace. Hitler preyed on the nation's sense of frustration, disappointment, and despair (Hoffer, 1989). Leni Riefenstahl's film documentary of Nazism was aptly entitled *Triumph of the Will*.

What is any government really but a parasitic growth, a group of old men who have set themselves up as a tax-collecting machine and who spend their time finding ways to run other people's lives? What if I choose not to accept them as my rulers? Is there any rational argument that can be brought to bear against my decision? Ultimately I might decide that submitting to a government is better than living without one, but there is nevertheless something slightly insulting in being told what to do by a group of people with whom I have never even signed a contract. When the economy is running smoothly, our politicians are quick to take the credit. When it is not running smoothly, they are quick to tell us that it is not their affair.

A major problem is that modern countries are often too large for effective democratic government. Yet neither military power nor economic well-being is necessarily correlated with the size of the political unit. Switzerland, for example, can hardly be considered either weak or impoverished. Schumacher (1989) claims that the relationship between the size of a nation and its well-being is actually an inverse one.

The so-called democratic nations of modern times face a self-contradiction: the word *democracy* means "government by the people," yet the average person has virtually no influence on the legislative, judicial, or administrative processes of the country. The concept of ascending levels of government, of representative government, sounds fine as a general idea, but in practice the average American's effect on Washington is miniscule.

In any case, governments, in the usual sense of the word, can hardly be said to govern anymore. It would be more accurate to say that it is corporations that rule the world, aided by clandestine plutocracies such as the World Trade Organization and the World Bank. The members of those corporations or plutocracies do not obtain their positions by means of a public election.

The tribe is generally more efficient than the empire. Any political party that was at all honest in its dealings would state quite plainly that the human population must drop from 7 billion to several million. What is needed is less Marx and Friedman, and more Schumacher—neither communism nor capitalism has done the world much good, and it is time to borrow something from the author of *Small Is Beautiful*. Schumacher's solutions are couched in patronizing monosyllables about moral reawakening, but he is on the right track. His dreams complement those of Peter Kropotkin (1968), a nine-teenth-century Russian advocate of syndicalism, anarchism, and non-violent revolution. They both envision a world without a corrupt and inefficient government, a world not covered with concrete and asphalt, a world that leaves room for trees and birds.

China, with a population of well over a billion, is hoping to develop an automobile industry as big as that of the US (Greider, 1998). All over the world, in fact, the have-nots are planning to join the haves. The dilemma is that if all other humans live like rich Americans, the Earth's problems of pollution and resource-consumption will be several times greater than they are already. It is hard to imagine the environmental effects of doubling the present number of automobiles. There is no resolution to the paradox, because it is a matter of mathematics: there is no way for the Earth to support more than a small fraction of the present number of people adequately. The present 7 billion is already so great that terrible famines get little coverage in a newspaper. Without severe population reduction, all talk of sustainable development is just fashionable chit-chat. Perhaps the reduction in population will never occur without a visit from the Four Horsemen of the Apocalypse.

To the extent that empires have formed vast cycles of expansion and decline, one can compare the present-day US to a world of many centuries ago. In the year 731, the Venerable Bede wrote his *Ecclesiastical History of the English People*, describing the world of the Heptarchy, the Seven Kingdoms of Kent, Wessex, Essex, Northumbria, East Anglia, Mercia, and Sussex. Bede was a monk in the monastery of Jarrow in Northumbria, and his *History* is dedicated to Ceolwulf, the king of that land. In his final chapter ("Chronological Recapitulation"), he tells us "in the year 409 [actually 410] Rome was brought down of the Goths; from which time the Romans ceased to rule in Britain" (Bede, 1962).

The fall of the Roman Empire has been ascribed to many things—poor leadership, general laziness, immorality, and so on. The impoverishment of the soil, and the consequent lack of food, may have played a part, as Lucretius suggests in Book 2 of *De Rerum Natura* (cf. chap. 9 of Carter and Dale, 1974). J. M. Roberts (1992) says that it was largely a military problem: the Roman Empire had grown enormous, and there just wasn't enough gold to pay for all those soldiers. Whatever the reason, in 410 the Goths managed to sack Rome.

Yet the end of a world can be the start of something better. When Bede was writing, the Roman Empire was still slowly turning to rubble and dust, but England's "Dark Ages" were filled with light, as the monks scratched away in their scriptoria. Although there were internal problems, Northumbria had had no major battles with the Picts, the Irish, or the Britons for decades, since King Ecgfrith had suffered a serious defeat by the Picts at the Battle of Dun Nechtain in 685, and apparently it was the Picts who killed King Osred in 716. In his penultimate chapter, Bede tells us that in the year 731 there was "the pleasantness of peace and quiet times." On a planet so primitive that even such basic problems as war, overpopulation, and government have not been solved, like Bede we can keep alive the miracle of reading and writing.

14
The End of Education

Teachers often jokingly say that the main function of
schools is to mop up unemployment, but in recent years
that may be truer than ever. The first element of the
"mopping up" is that in today's schools almost nothing
is taught and almost nothing is learned. Secondly, even
if that were not the case, there are no jobs for those who
clutch their diplomas and go out into the streets. The
third element of the mopping up, perhaps slightly more
beneficial to all concerned, is that schools at least manage to separate children from their parents. The latter
might even be employed, although probably underpaid,
but if they do have jobs they barely have time to breathe,
let alone take care of their children. Let us look at these
three elements more closely.

Educational standards throughout the world reached
rock bottom several years ago, and now there is really
no such thing as passing or failing. The discarding of
testing began in the liberal '60s, but that was a world in
which it almost made sense to do that, since utopia was
then imaginable, and perhaps even tangible. It was not
the economic cauldron of the twenty-first century. Instead of standards of any real sort, what we have now is
the absurdity of "compulsory" education without the

compulsion—without the tests that would reinforce any of that learning. (The wisdom of compulsory education is itself very much open to question. In an ideal world, would there really be such a thing?) If the students decide to mutiny, there is nothing the teachers can do about it, and if those teachers report the matter they are likely to be fired for incompetence. It may be fortunate for the teachers that the students are unaware of how much power for destruction they really have.

The second point mentioned above is that there are no jobs for graduates, and since that is the case, it may be a waste of time to educate them. The unemployment problem is now ultimately based on the permanent decline in the world's resources, but it actually began with globalization in the late twentieth century: the more advanced a country, the more likely it was that the multinational corporations would export the jobs to countries where workers were paid lower wages. Even then, the main goal was to replace the workers with computers and other forms of machinery. Now, however, since the world's economy has been suffering for years from an imbalance between population and resources, especially fossil fuels and metals, no worker anywhere can count on keeping a job. There seems to be a tacit understanding that there is no point in enforcing high standards of education if that learning cannot be put to use in the outside world. We need not assume that there is some sort of "global conspiracy" to destroy the human mind: economic forces alone can do it.

The third and final point, as mentioned above, is that the schools are busy keeping children off the streets because the parents are too busy trying to make a living, even if their jobs keep them only at the survival level, whereas in the 1950s only one parent needed to have a job. Knowing that there are others standing in line, workers always live in fear of losing their jobs, and they willingly work at high-level tasks for low-level pay. The old standard of full-time permanent occupations has been replaced by temporary work, no matter what euphemisms may be applied to such jobs. Even then, the modern couple is heavily in debt and facing an uncertain future. For those parents who are completely unemployed, there may be more time to spare, but that idleness can hardly be said to produce happiness.

Today's teacher is therefore just a babysitter. For one person to be in charge of 30 oversized babies can be quite an unpleasant situation, no matter how cost-effective it may be for society. For all the above reasons, there will be a demand for teachers for some time to come—or at least a shortage thereof. A recent graduate, however, might do well to choose a career path other than that of modern mis-education.

A final note to be added is that students might be aware of something the teachers have missed. It may, quite simply, be pointless trying to educate the average person, at least in the ordinary sense of the word, and one might even argue that that has always been the case. Most of what is called education is applicable only to a vanished world, or even to a world that never existed, and students seem to have some dim but genuine perception of the fact. There is no point in learning the geography of a country one will never be able to visit, or learning a language one will never have a chance to speak.

There are certainly skills that will be needed in the chaotic world of the future. I would even say that education for the real world begins with the principle that every teenager, at least in rural areas (where any sensible person would be living), should know how to use a rifle and an axe, since the first might provide food and the second might provide a home. A university degree that leaves its owner many thousands of dollars in debt, on the other hand, is not providing a foundation for survival in the coming times. The corollary is that education in such real-world skills cannot be acquired by sitting at a desk.

15
Crime in the Post-Peak World

As humanity plunges into the age of declining resources, what will be the future of crime? The particular problem of which I am thinking might be called, more specifically, "future violence," since other acts that are now considered criminal may seem trivial in later days. The topic is a huge and nebulous one, and the following notes can barely raise the questions, let alone provide the answers. Even a brief and random search of the available texts, however, may reveal a few patterns. Some of the information about this topic, incidentally, comes from anonymous sources at the grassroots level, indicating the extent to which those in high places sometimes evade responsibility.

There can certainly be a good deal of nastiness to human behaviour. One reason for violence is that it can be one of life's greatest pleasures: fighting can be quite an emotional relief, and as primary a need as eating or sleeping; many men have come home from war and spent decades boring the next generation with tales of conquest (Kaplan, 1994, February). An anonymous police officer, in an essay entitled "The Thin Blue Line," claims that man is by nature cruel, always looking for opportunities for selfishness and evil, and that it is wiser to accept that the day will come when that evil must be faced (Deputy W., 2009, January). In particular, violent crime becomes imminent when the "authorities" are weak or absent: that is the difference between Ireland in the potato famine of the 1840s and a credit collapse like that of lawless Argentina in 2001.

A rise in criminal behaviour apparently began a few decades ago. In the foreword to Green's *Crime and Civil Society*, Judge Alan Taylor says, with reference to the UK, that there has been a great increase in crime over the years, but that much of it goes unreported (Green, Grove, & Martin, 2005). Even during natural disasters, the extent of crime seems to be misreported in the press. A witness to the Hurricane Katrina disaster in 2005 mentions that problems of law enforcement were often ignored, and that the news media were often denied information about incidents. Police officers were angry about the frequent cover-ups, and about the falsification of statistics (Anonymous, 2007, February 13).

It seems that in the future there will be little difference between crime and warfare (Kaplan, 1994, February). Even at present, war is often no longer between state and state but closer to a world in which the state as such does not exist. Mercenaries often fight on their own behalf, to such an extent that the distinction between armies and the populace is unclear, and the rules of engagement are likely to be non-existent.

No doubt the police will be overburdened in the coming decades, in view of the fact that even now the police force is inadequate for accommodating present levels of crime. In a condition of true social collapse, there will be greater opportunities for crime, while conversely the police force will be unable to increase its numbers, partly because the money to do so will be unavailable.

Fuel supplies will be tightly rationed, perhaps almost unavailable to those who do not constitute "authorities," but eventually even those people will be facing a shortage. The sight of police cars sitting in a police-station parking lot, with no fuel to put those cars on the road, would be quite funny if it were not so foreboding. And a police force trying to operate during a lengthy breakdown of the electric-power grid might not be able to do much of anything.

When the economy collapses, and many are facing unemployment, a point is reached at which everyone is concerned about the shortage of food, water, and shelter. Another concern will be for the protection of the immediate family. If at the present time there are only enough police officers to deal with the more-important crimes, in the future it will become apparent to such officers that they too need to be at home and protecting their own families (Deputy W., 2009, January).

The observer of the Hurricane Katrina disaster has little positive to say about any authorities that became involved in that event. His impression was that the best plan was to form a group and divide the various tasks. One irony was that those who were better prepared were threatened by the less prepared, whose attitude was that the former must have unfairly done better. Later, when authorities actually arrived, they were likely to go beyond the letter of the law and demand unreasonable obedience even from those who had no wish or need to be saved (Anonymous, 2007, February 13).

Crime fighting in the future will be further complicated by the ambiguity of the "bad guys." Powerful weapons are not of much use when it is not clear at whom one should be shooting, and this enigma has been around for decades. American soldiers in Vietnam were often plagued by not knowing who constituted the enemy. The trend is certainly toward urban warfare and away from the more-clearly defined battlegrounds of earlier times.

The police in Western society hold a position that is in many ways paradoxical or ambiguous. There is a common belief that modern democracies are blessed with law and order, but sometimes the reality is otherwise: if my house is robbed, the police will arrive eventually and take notes, but that may be all they will do, or can do.

The main function of the police, we are often told, is to preserve the peace. But exactly *whose* peace is it that they are preserving? Perhaps "preserving the peace" simply means ensuring that the common people do not disturb the basic structure of society. It often seems that the point of a crime investigation is not to come to the aid of the victim, but merely to see who is trying to rock the boat. In most cases the suspect is nobody worth worrying about. Such matters as ordinary assault and robbery do nothing to damage the walls of the empire, so the police will simply add the case to the files and forget about it.

The police themselves are not entirely to blame for their inability to aid society. They can be held accountable if they believe that any political ignorance on their own part is justifiable as political neutrality, but greater problems are caused by irrational laws and an overburdened judiciary. When governments deliberately lie about crime figures, and when the courts are perpetually buffeted by the shifting winds of politics, even the most enlightened and well-meaning police officer is in a difficult situation.

The questionable role of the police becomes most obvious in the evolution of the "surveillance society." The miracle of modern communications has its nefarious side: the electronic utopia of the future would be one of transponders, closed-circuit television, helicopters, and forbidden zones, or perhaps less-anachronistic variations thereof. For whose good is this being done? Who is being protected from whom? Fortunately the problem contains its own solution: technophilia is a disease for which time is the best remedy. As fuel, metals, and electricity go into decline, such weaponry will no longer be available for use against the general population.

When it is far too late, we may realize how much we have lost. In the modern world, many ridicule their own inherited political ideals, but they may misunderstand the difference between those ideals and the present conditions. Democracy, equal rights, civil liberty, the rule of law, and so on cannot be explained clearly in less than a few hundred pages. The people who disparage those ideals are generally those who have enjoyed living in that world since the day they were born, and they are unaware of the reality of life under other regimes except as temporary vacationers at an American-owned hotel.

16
Why Nobody Is Listening

There are several reasons why talk of systemic collapse sometimes doesn't get much response, but one clue to the puzzle may be the grimness of the survivalist image. "Man Alone" with his AK-47 and his lifetime supply of pork and beans has little relation to reality: a loner can never defeat a mob, and all it takes is one bullet to end that sort of battle. At best, the story of Man Alone is true only as allegory. Nevertheless, there's a question, and there's an answer, even if the two somehow don't match. The answer, or at least the final remark, is "the horror," as Conrad has his character say in *Heart of Darkness*.

Times have changed. Four teenagers in an old car with broken suspension and rolled-down windows cruise the streets, shouting obscenities at lone pedestrians. A young lady with an enormous student loan tells me she knows she'll never be able to pay it off. A fellow teacher with whom I'm supposed to be working keeps falling asleep: her neighbour had an all-night party, and it's the middle of the week. She says, "There's nothing you can do about it." I know: the police barely have the staff to handle major crimes. And, yes, it's true: sometimes they feel there's not much rewarding about their jobs.

Crime, cults, craziness, and chaos. Every day we add another 200,000 to the world's population. Every day, most of the world's natural resources go further into decline. It's an insane inversion of Maslow's hierarchy of needs: everything from the material to the spiritual is in short supply.

Why is nobody listening? Five reasons, beginning with the fact that it's not really "nobody." There are many people who know the world is going down the drain. They may not know exactly how, but they know. They may not speak, but they know.

Secondly, the entire problem is too multidimensional. How can any theorist pin together all the connections from peak oil to peak chaos? And even if the connections could be made, how could they be explained? And the problem is increased by the fact that the average American spends two and a half hours a day watching television. How many hours does that leave for any genuine research?

Thirdly, there is a mountain of disinformation out there. All those "environmental" organizations were supposed to be saving the spotted whatever, but they were getting funds from the corporations that committed the crimes. And then there are the economists, who think the most distant galaxy can be explained solely in terms of money. Looking at prices is misleading, because the problem is not a matter of money, but of geology: when it takes two barrels of oil to get one barrel of oil out of the ground, any further drilling would be just a waste of time. And every six months, the magazines at the checkout counter announce "the miracle of x energy," as if the previous "miracle" had never happened. And any mention of overpopulation, of course, brings five or six major religions down on one's neck. We may be overloaded with data, but we're not overloaded with genuine information.

Fourthly, those who claim to have all the answers don't really have them, and I'm probably as guilty as anyone. I have no idea how 7 billion people can fit on a planet designed for 10 million. All I do know is that a great many people are going to die in the process of adjusting those numbers. Of course, that's not an answer either, so certainly no one is going to listen to that.

But I think, above all, that the reason no one is listening is that even those who know "the answer" aren't going to put it into words. It's just too hard to say. It will be the Gunfight at the O. K. Corral. That's what we don't like to say. That's what the "survivalist" nuts have been saying for years, but those of us who are more refined simply dismiss them as loud-mouthed yahoos. There's no faster way of getting oneself ostracized in polite society than by talking about guns. But I think I can see how Doc Holliday gave up dentistry: he had to face "the horror." People who talk about "doom and gloom" fall into two camps: blue-collar and white-collar. The blue-collar group uses the word *survival* a lot and is obsessed with off-road vehicles, guns, and wilderness living. The white-collar group is obsessed with writing to their legislators, while rolling their eyes at any mention of conflict.

The end product of chaos will be widespread violence. That's exactly what the "lowbrows" have been saying for years. It's just unfortunate that the "highbrows" haven't been listening, or that they've been too squeamish to deal with the question. That violence is what I am referring to when I mention the O. K. Corral—which, oddly enough, was a microcosm of our present problems of overpopulation, immigration, and ethnic conflict: it was a struggle between cowboys and farmers for a finite piece of land.

Or perhaps I should say, the reason why it seems that nobody is listening is simply that nobody wants to say what everyone's been thinking. What everyone's been thinking is not so much that the lowbrows don't deserve to be right, but that the highbrows have spent their lives with no defences at all, either physical or emotional. (I am reminded, in that respect, of the two races of posthumans in H. G. Wells's *The Time Machine*.) I'm not advocating "the horror." I'm merely predicting it, at least to the extent that I can legitimize my role as disinterested observer. In any case, if I actually had to kill anybody, I think I'd go into a trauma for six months.

Definitely, being a loner is not going to work for most people, in spite of all the Wild West movies about such characters. Maybe dealing with "the horror" means thinking again about that gunfight in Tombstone, Arizona. Wyatt Earp had three brothers with him, as well his friend Doc Holliday. Those numbers made a big difference, I'm sure. There were five people who utterly trusted one another. Of course, if you're really looking for a tribe to belong to, then a slightly larger group would be better.

17
Peak Oil and Global Warming

To what extent, if any, will reductions in the availability of oil and other fossil fuels reduce the problem of global warming? Some uncertainty about climate change is due to the many complexities and synergies of the atmosphere itself. Other uncertainty is due to the question of how much the human race will consciously attempt to mitigate the problems. Even more, however, is due to the question of how fast the world's fossil fuels will run out, with or without any conscious attempt to reduce the use of such fuels.

It seems most likely that peak oil is around 2010, give or take a few years. It seems that peak coal will be about 2020 or 2025, much sooner than indicated by previous scenarios. There is little that needs to be said about less-conventional fossil fuels, except that much of the public relations are designed to trap foolhardy investors.

The possible atmospheric side effects of peak fuels, both upwards and downwards, are numerous. Overpopulation in itself creates many dangers simply by increasing the use of fuels of all types. Declines in fuels will no doubt cause a severe decline in the global economy, perhaps even a downward spiral, and the lower the economy, the lower the emissions. But then a badly damaged economy could create tensions leading to war, which would have its own environmental effects. There could also be problems with deforestation, caused in part by a greater use of wood for heating fuel, but also by a need to clear land for agriculture, and every tree destroyed adds CO_2 to the atmosphere. Eventually, though, the decline in fuels, combined with a generally poor economy, will lead to famine and a consequent decline in population.

In any case, it is evident that the temperature of the planet has increased by about 0.6 °C since about 1860, almost certainly because of the burning of fossil fuels. The future increase in temperature, over the entire course of the twenty-first century, is less easy to determine. In the words of the Intergovernmental Panel on Climate Change's *Special Report: Emissions Scenarios* (IPCC, 2000), "Future greenhouse gas (GHG) emissions are the product of very complex dynamic systems . . . . Their future evolution is highly uncertain." According to the IPCC's *Fourth Assessment Report* (IPCC, 2007), the global climate over the course of the twenty-first century will probably increase by somewhere between 1.1 and 6.4 °C—a rather large range of estimates.

As the temperature goes up, feedback mechanisms come into play. As ice melts, for example, less radiation is reflected back into space, so there is an additional rise in temperature. As the tundra heats up, carbon and methane are released, causing a further rise in temperature. The question is: At what point do these cycles go out of control? This point is sometimes referred to as dangerous anthropogenic interference (DAI), and it is generally estimated to be at CO_2 concentrations of somewhere between 450 ppm and 550 ppm.

The IPCC reports indicate a variety of emissions scenarios, and the models they present are only a selection of the possible futures. Nevertheless, the IPCC generally tends to downplay the likelihood that fossil fuels of all types will be in decline well before the middle of the century.

On the other hand, Pushker Kharecha and James Hansen (2007, April 26) claim that an early decline in the use of fossil fuels would result in peak CO_2 concentrations at somewhere between 422 and 440 ppm, far below the dangerous levels shown in other scenarios. James Lovelock (2007, September 6) believes that future emissions scenarios in general are exaggerated. Kjell Aleklett (2007, June 5) is convinced that reasonable estimates of fossil-fuel decline indicate future temperature estimates that are generally much lower than those of the IPCC.

All of the above, of course, is not meant to imply that the future climate will be trouble-free. Between one monster and another there may not be much to choose. We can, however, at least hope that the reduction in fossil fuels can mitigate some of the problems of global warming.

18
Leadership and Social Structure

The story of the imminent collapse of industrial civilization rarely appears in the conventional news media, or it appears only in distorted forms. Ironically, the modern world is plagued by a lack of serious information. Today's news item is usually forgotten by tomorrow. The television viewer has the vague impression that something happened somewhere, but one could change channels all day without finding anything below the surface. The communications media are owned by an ever-shrinking number of interrelated giant corporations, and the product sold to the public is a uniform blandness, designed to keep the masses in their place (Bagdikian, 2004; McChesney, 2004). But the unreality of television is only the start of the enigma. The larger problem is that there is no leadership, no sense of organization, for dealing with the important issues.

One might consider as an analogy the Great Depression. During those 10 years, everyone lived on a separate island, lost, alone, and afraid. It was a "shame" to be poor, so one could not even discuss it with the neighbours. The press and the politicians largely denied that the Depression existed, so there was little help from them. In general, it was just each nuclear family on its own—for those who were lucky enough to have a family (Broadfoot, 1997).

As the oil crisis worsens there will be various forms of aberrant behaviour: denial, anger, mental paralysis. There will be an increase in crime; there will be extremist political movements. Strange religious cults will arise; "fundamentalists" are already on the rise everywhere (Catton, 1982; Thurow, 1996). The reason for such behaviour is that the peak-oil problem is really neither about economics nor about politics. Nor is it about alternative energy; there's no such thing. It's about geology. It's about humanity's attempt to defy geology. But it's also about psychology: most people cannot grasp the concept of "overshoot" (Catton, 1982).

We cannot come to terms with the fact that as a species we have gone beyond the ability of the planet to accommodate us. We have bred ourselves beyond the limits. We have consumed, polluted, and expanded beyond our means, and after centuries of superficial technological solutions, we are now running short of answers. Biologists explain such expansion in terms of "carrying capacity." Lemmings and snowshoe hares—and a great many other species—have the same problem; overpopulation and overconsumption lead to die-off. But humans cannot come to terms with the concept. It goes against the grain of all our religious and philosophical beliefs.

When we were children, nobody told us that any of this would be happening. Nobody told us that the human spirit would have to face limitations. We were taught that there are no necessary boundaries to human achievement. We were taught that optimism, realism, and exuberance are just three names for the same thing. In a philosophical sense, therefore, most humans never become adults: they cannot understand limits.

Perhaps there is really nothing irredeemable in all this. We live in a "consumer" society, and we are all under the wheels of the juggernaut of capitalism. But if we look beyond civilization, both spatially and temporally, we can find many cultures with an outlook based more on the seasons of the year, rather than on an ever-expanding, ever-devouring "progress."

19
The Post-Oil Community

It's easy to say, "Let's form a community and deal with the post-oil economy." An ad-hoc social group of any sort often sounds like a great thing to be starting, but often they don't work. What happens is roughly as follows. Each member has a vague dislike of most other members: after all, they may have nothing in common except the one thing the group came together for. Most people don't want to do any work to help the organization: administration (typing, filing, phoning) is boring. At meetings, most people don't speak, since they're afraid of starting a big argument, but they'll gather privately and complain for weeks afterwards. Everyone assumes that when officers have been elected, the other members can all forget about the organization; for the rest of the year, if there are any problems, then "They" should fix them. When everything starts to fall apart, some rather manipulative person jumps into the vacuum and establishes a dictatorship; soon afterward, the membership is down to zero.

Why do these problems occur, and how will people form viable groups in the future? To answer these questions properly, we first must realize that the ideal political system is not a "political" matter at all, but a psychological one. What I mean is that it is not a conscious, cerebral decision; it is a matter of the hard-wiring of our nervous system. And I say that as one who does not believe in evolutionary psychology or sociobiology, or any other of those antlike portrayals of human mentality. Humans and their ancestors spent about 2 million years living in small groups, hunting and gathering. To judge from primitive societies that still exist, those groups had neither perfect dictatorship nor pure democracy, but something in the middle, a sort of semi-anarchic but functional process of majority rule; chiefs who didn't perform well got the cold shoulder (Ferguson, 2003, July/August; Lee, 1968; Harris, 1989).

The group was small enough that each person knew every other person, and the rather clumsy democracy could work because both the "voters" and the "politicians" were visible. It has only been in a tiny fraction of the lifespan of humanity—the period called *civilization*—that political units have been created that are far too large for people to know one another except as abstractions. Small groups have their problems, but in terms of providing happiness for the average person, the band or village has always been more efficient than the empire.

The maximum practical size for human association may be Robin Dunbar's number of 150 (1992), but we might need to be rather flexible about that—perhaps somewhere between about 20 and 200. Roman soldiers, for example, were organized into "centuries," and modern Hutterite communities have between 60 and 160 members. The same was true long before the Romans: a

Paleolithic pack included about 20 or 30 people, whereas in Neolithic times a village might have a population of 150 or more (Starr, 1991).

But a close look at half a dozen types of human groups is all that is necessary to get a good intuitive grasp of the sorts of numbers that are workable. Groups larger than that of the band or the small tribe simply do not do as well in providing for the happiness of their individual members. A social group of a million or a billion may have military advantages but is more likely to operate as a tyranny than as a democracy—China is the obvious case. Larger groups are not necessarily unworkable, but they involve a greater risk of the loss of social cohesion.

It is the problem of "individualism" versus "collectivism" that will hit Americans rather hard in the future. Americans are loners. After years of living and working with people from various Eastern cultures, I am convinced that if you put a group of Asians on a desert island, they would get together and build a boat. If you put a group of Caucasian Americans on a desert island, they would start arguing about property rights.

Closely related to the problem of individualism is that of the lack of ideological unity. The basic premises of any major discussion seem to be absent. In a typical crowd of Americans, half will deny that any of the aspects of systemic collapse even exist, and most of the other half will say, "Well, I believe . . ." and proceed to spout whatever nonsense their brains have been filled with. If politicians never say a word about overpopulation, resource consumption, or any other real issue, how can the average person be blamed for mental laziness? But perhaps there's something to be said for intellectual responsibility. Certainly no one can say that informative books aren't available.

The individualist mentality has always been typical of Americans. There is a sort of frontier mentality that still pervades much of American life. In certain ways, this has been beneficial: freedom from the obligations of the "old country" has provided much of the motivation for those who came to what was called the New World. The beneficial side of individualism is self-sufficiency, which made it possible for pioneers to survive in the isolation of the wilderness. But individualism will not be as useful a response in the future as it was in pioneer times. In fact, individualism might just be more beneficial in good times than in bad, in times of prosperity rather than in times of hardship. There are, admittedly, a few people who have both the skills and the fortitude for independent living, but for the great majority the future will require a sense of community.

The most obvious negative effect of individualism can be seen in today's false democracy: political leaders can tell the most remarkable lies, and the response is silent obedience. It is hard to understand such a thing happening in "the land of the free and the home of the brave" until we realize that most Americans have little means of behaving otherwise. They are probably lacking in family or friends with whom they can share information or compare ideas, and they therefore depend on the mainstream news media for their comprehension of human society. A solitary evening in front of a television set is not likely to promote healthy social relationships.

One cannot throw a "tribe" together simply by sitting down and having a community chat in the course of one afternoon in a suburban living room. (The fact that we don't instantly recognize something so obvious is in itself evidence of our inability to form a "tribe.") Primitive cultures may be organized into any of a number of social groupings, and those groupings in turn are often parts of a larger group—there is a pyramidal structure. But there are two characteristics that are found in these primitive cultures. In the first place, the group is always quite ancient; any group of that sort has been forming and reforming for countless generations, and one might say that the group is as old as humanity. Secondly, any genuine social group in a primitive society consists of members who are all tied by the bonds of either blood or marriage. Everybody is everybody else's cousin, so to speak. We may laugh at rural communities for what we regard as their "incestuous" behaviour, but sometimes having close ties is precisely what keeps people alive.

In any large-scale disaster, in which help is needed quickly, group members get chosen from whoever is useful: the most knowledgeable, those with the best social skills, or perhaps just the nearest. In the long run, however, what will prevail will be the family, as it always has done. In a primitive society, most social divisions begin with the family, although more important is not the nuclear family but the extended one. Nuclear families are somewhat temporary, whereas the extended family is timeless. From the family comes the idea of descent from those in the past, and it reaches outward in the present to all the aunts and uncles and so on. The family may be traced through the fathers, or through the mothers, or both.

If the family is large enough, and descent is reckoned through a very distant ancestor, anthropologists may refer to it as a clan; the ancestor may be mythical, though, perhaps even taking the form of an animal or a god. If several clans (called moieties if there are only two) live together, or at least associate with one another in some way such as intermarriage, the larger group is called a phratry. If the community is large enough, with formal concepts of social rank and leadership, it may be labelled a tribe. (There is no definition of *tribe* that suits all scholars, but often there is the notion of a group larger than a mere band, with a more-elaborate social structure and a more formal leadership.) But always the foundation of these social groups is the mating of a man and a woman, and the children that come from that bond.

The terms describing systems of kinship have enormous variation in meaning from one society to another, but in all cases these labels signify the ties from one individual to another, beginning with the husband and wife and extending out in all directions. The ties are always either those of blood or marriage, but marriage makes one an honorary member of that society. Each tie is emotional, not just some sort of business relationship.

The traditional social group, then, is characterized both by its antiquity and by its kinship patterns. Such patterns would certainly not be characteristic of a group of suburbanite refugees lost in the wilderness and suffering from shock and fatigue. It would be an understatement to say that such an ad-hoc clustering of humans would face psychological challenges unlike those of people who had been living deep in the jungle since time immemorial.

It should be obvious that those who live in the country will be better prepared than those who live in cities. A city is a place that consumes a great deal but produces little in terms of life's essentials. A city without incoming food or water collapses rapidly, whereas a small community closely tied to the natural environment can more easily adjust to technological and economic troubles. Even out in the country, however, the present housing patterns often resemble the gasoline-induced sprawl of the suburbs. Paradoxically, many "rural" areas have become "urbanized," in the sense that they are doing their best to imitate the worst aspects of large cities. More useful would be something resembling a traditional village, with the houses at the focus and the fields radiating from that point. We can read Thomas Hardy's novels to get a feeling of how this used to be.

"Something resembling a traditional village" is different from the real thing. In a genuine "traditional village," people have known one another for generations, and a crowd of urban visitors is not likely to be received with open arms. If these refugees show up flashing their useless credit cards all over the place, and demanding assistance, but they have no practical skills and do not even have the muscles for basic manual labour, it is unlikely that they will be welcomed in any long-settled community. These refugees will have to develop their own communities, and they will have to overcome the problem of their inadequate social skills. But some will learn—in spite of themselves.

If a post-oil community actually got underway, one thing to be avoided, for the most part, would be the issue of "division of labour"—dividing up jobs or professions: farmers, carpenters, etc. In most primitive societies, most people were good at most things. There was a vague division along the lines of gender and age, but that was about it, and even that was by no means absolute. Any future community would have to behave in the same manner as most primitive societies. And it would certainly be a "primitive society": if no one in the community had ever produced a crop of beans successfully, there would be little point in worrying about an elaborate division of labour.

By the end of the present century, the human population will be much smaller than it is now. The two-hundred-odd nations of the present day will be only a dim memory. Grass will be growing everywhere, and the long kilometres of cracked highways will be merely a curiosity. Starlight will once again appear over the cities at night. Humans were not designed to live in groups of such immense size as we see today, nor were they given the physiological equipment to deal with the overstimulation of crowded living spaces. It is also true, for various reasons, that the sight of green trees is more pleasing than that of grey machines. It is not just a platitude to say that we are out of touch with Nature.

20
The Widening Spiral

As mundane as it may seem in our "advanced" civilization, peak oil basically means peak food. Farmers are invisible people, and middle-class city dwellers choose to pretend that the long lines of trucks bringing food into the city at dawn every day have nothing to do with the white-collar world. Perhaps it is a mark of the civilized person to believe that the essentials of food, clothing, and shelter have no relevance to daily life. Yet if the farmers stopped sending food into the great vacuum of the metropolis, the great maw of urbanity, the city would rapidly crumble, as Britain discovered during the transport strike of the year 2000 (McMahon, 2006, August 21). The next question, then, is: where does all this food come from?

Is there such a thing as sustainable agriculture, or is *sustainable agriculture* an oxymoron? To keep a piece of land producing crops, it is necessary to maintain a high level of various elements. The most critical are phosphorus (P), potassium (K), and especially nitrogen (N). These elements might be abundant in the soil before any cultivation is done, but they are removed to some extent whenever crops are harvested.

Writing early in the twentieth century, F. H. King

(n.d.) claimed that farmers in China, Japan, and Korea were managing to grow abundant crops on about one tenth as much cultivable land per capita as Americans, and that they had done so for 4,000 years. If they kept their land producing for all those centuries, what was their secret? The answer, in part, is that most of eastern Asia has an excellent climate, with rainfall most abundant when it is most needed. More importantly, agriculture was sustained by the practice of returning almost all waste to the soil—even human excrement from the cities was carried long distances to the farms. Various legumes, grown in the fields between the planting of food crops, fixed atmospheric nitrogen in the soil. Much of the annually depleted N-P-K, however, was replaced by taking vegetation from the hillsides and mountains, and by the use of silt, which was taken from the irrigation canals but which originated in the mountains. The system, therefore, was not a closed one, because it took materials from outside the farms.

These three countries are, in any case, problematic as sources of agricultural "wisdom." King remarks that "the first days of travel in these old countries force the over-crowding upon the attention as nothing else can" (p. 23). In a chapter on Tientsin, he cites a Scottish physician's description of a common solution to overcrowding: "In times of famine the girls especially are disposed of, often permitted to die when very young for lack of care. Many are sold at such times to go into other provinces" (p. 331). As for the hard labour and low remuneration, King says of a Japanese rice farmer that "it is difficult for Americans to understand how it is possible for the will of man, even when spurred by the love of home and family, to hold flesh to tasks like these" (p. 209). The "miracle" of growing so much food on so little land was largely due, therefore, to neither technology nor topography, but to the fact that starvation was the only alternative.

In some societies, agriculture meant slow but inexorable burnout, as was the case for most of Europe. In other cultures (e.g., China, Japan, and Korea) the response was to recycle intensively. As much as possible, vegetable compost and human and animal excrement had to be reclaimed. Other loss was made up by importing soil and vegetation from the wilderness. Even for those cultures a growing population exacerbated the problems.

World agriculture faces the problem of a reduction in arable land, but there is also the problem of water. The natural availability of water has always been one of the most critical factors in farming. Most of the western US receives only 50 cm or less rainfall annually. But low precipitation is a problem in parts of every continent. In a real survival situation, what are the chances that anyone would be able to pick up a plastic hose and get an endless supply of clear cold water? Not very great. Even wells, cisterns, and ponds would be useless if their water flow had been controlled by electricity. When water must be pumped by hand or carried in buckets, it becomes a precious commodity.

But the world's food problems cannot be solved merely by devising a method to increase agriculture. The world's human population is now over 7 billion, while the amount of arable land is not great. Massive inputs of artificial fertilizers and pesticides only replace one problem with others: poisoned water, eroded soil, and insufficient humus. Even the world's present arable land is rapidly disappearing under cities and highways. Nor can we extend that land by pumping more water from underground, because the aquifers cannot be made to yield more water than they receive.

There may be something resembling sustainability, depending partly on one's definitions, but it would have little to do with the simplistic concepts that are usually put forward. In the first place, there is nothing "natural" about agriculture. Agriculture has only been practiced for less than one percent of the entire history of our genus, and in that sense it is still an experiment with uncertain results. To plow the earth is to "go against Nature," since it means disturbing the soil, the intricate, complex surface of the planet. The slightest and shallowest disturbance causes chemical and biological losses of various sorts. The Paleolithic practice of foraging, with a greatly reduced population, may be the only way of life that can be extended for millennia (Ferguson, 2003, July/August; Lee, 1968). Nevertheless, with such a large global population it is certain that agriculture will continue for at least the next few decades, and in the absence of fossil fuels the majority of survivors will be working their individual plots of land.

In spite of the dangers of perpetual growth in agricultural production, in some countries one can drive for days without seeing an end to cultivated land (or asphalt and concrete). Almost no attention is paid to the final consequences of such practices, and the relentless quest for money makes it unlikely that serious attention will ever be paid. Even on a theoretical level, the permanent feeding of humanity is not simple. Any long-term solution would require paying as much attention to restoration of the land as has previously been paid to its cultivation.

Secondly and more importantly, to maintain a somewhat-permanent balance between population and cultivation would require a considerable reduction in the former. It is foolish to say that the gap between food and population can be met by increasing the production of food. The error, a rather obvious one, is that an increase in food is inevitably followed by a further increase in population, which in turn leads to another shortage of food. Since the dawn of the human race, people have been trying to find ways to increase the food supply; often they have succeeded. Perhaps the biggest innovation of all was agriculture itself, the discovery that one can deliberately put seeds into the ground and foster their growth, rather than going off into the jungle to look for plants growing in the wild. That particular revolution led to a great increase in human population. The original problem, however, simply recurred. The solution (some means of increasing food) always leads straight back to the original problem (an excess population).

But these two forces do not act merely in a circular fashion. It would be more exact to say that they act as an ever-widening spiral. If we double the food supply, and thereby induce a doubling of human population, the new problem (that of excessive population) is not entirely identical to the original problem, because as the spiral widens, it creates further dangers.

At some point, we will push the planet Earth to the point where it can no longer maintain that spiral. We can convert great quantities of petrochemicals into fertilizers and pesticides, and we can draw water out of the deepest aquifers and even desalinate the oceans, but at some point we have to face the fact that the Earth is only a rock small enough that a jet plane can encircle it in a matter of hours. We are squeezing both our residential areas and our farmlands beyond endurance. The greatest danger of such a spiral is that when it breaks, it will do so in a far more destructive way than if the problem had been solved earlier. When the human race suddenly finds itself unable to manage the reciprocity of overpopulation and food production, there will be no more choices left to make.

21
World Food Supplies

Only about 10 percent of the world's land surface is arable, whereas the other 90 percent is just rock, sand, or swamp, which can never be made to produce crops, whether we use "high" or "low" technology or something in the middle (Bot et al., 2000; CIA, 2010). In an age with diminishing supplies of oil and other fossil fuels, this 1:9 ratio may be creating two serious problems that have been largely ignored.

The first is that humans are not living only on that 10 percent of arable land, although that 10 percent is more densely populated than the rest. Humans are living everywhere, while trucks, trains, ships, and airplanes bring the food to where those people are living. When the vehicles are no longer operating, the people living in outlying regions will probably start moving into those "10 percent" lands where the crops can be grown.

The other problem with the 1:9 ratio is that with "low technology," i.e., technology that does not use petroleum or other fossil fuels, crop yields diminish considerably. With non-mechanized agriculture, corn (maize) production is only about 2,000 kilograms per hectare, less than a third of the yield that a farmer would get with modern machinery and chemical fertilizer (Pimentel, 1984). If that is the case, then not only will almost 100 percent of the people be living on the productive 10 percent of the land, but there will be much less food available for that 100 percent.

Oddly enough, if other crops are substituted for corn, there is usually no enormous difference in the number of kilocalories per hectare. Beans (as "dry beans") produce about half the yield of corn. Root crops (turnips, carrots, beets, etc.) are impressive in terms of their bulk—mass—per hectare, yet they do not differ greatly from corn in kilocalories per hectare.

Actually there is a third problem that arises from the first two. This is the fact that if 100 percent of the people are living on 10 percent of the land, then the land may have so many people, roads, and buildings on it that a good deal of that land will be unavailable for farming. This problem of disappearing farmland is not a new one, of course; for centuries it seemed only common sense to build our cities in the midst of our paradises.

Let us play with some of these numbers and see what happens. These are only rough figures, admittedly, but greater accuracy is impossible because of the question of how one defines one's terms, and even more by the fact that everything on this poor planet is rapidly changing. The present population of the Earth is now over 7 billion, and the number is rapidly increasing every day. That number should be large enough to make us seriously consider the consequences. (What other large mammal can be found in such numbers?) When I was born, in 1949, there were less than 3 billion people, and it amazes me that this jump to 7 billion is rarely regarded as significant. These 7 billion people live on the land surface of the Earth, which is about 150 million km^2 in area, but the arable land is only about 15 million km^2. The ratio of people to km^2 is therefore about 470:1, or less than 5 per hectare.

Are those numbers a matter for concern? I would think so. As we saw earlier, with pre-industrial technology, a hectare of corn would support, at the utmost, only 9 people, or in other words 1 km^2 would support no more than 900 people.

That number probably does not closely resemble reality. Beside the problem of roads and buildings taking up space, allowances would have to be made for fallow land, and perhaps for the production of green manure (crops grown as compost). One would have to ensure that the land was both logically and equitably distributed. The 1:9 ratio is also assuming no increase in population, although famine and the attendant decrease in fertility will take care of that matter very soon. A separate issue is the question: after decades of agribusiness, how much of the world's supposedly arable land is really as fertile and healthy as in earlier times?

The average entire house lot in the US is about 1,000 m^2. That is one tenth of the minimum amount of land required to feed nine people. But even if every square metre of our planet's "arable portion" were devoted to the raising of corn or other useful crops, we would have serious trouble trying to feed an average of nine people from each hectare of arable land.

Given such figures, one should beware of writers

who are liberal in their use of such words as *alternative*, *sustainable*, and *transition*. Simple arithmetic is all that is needed to show that such terminology is not applicable to the situation.

Nor am I convinced when proponents of "organic gardening" claim they can grow unlimited amounts of food merely by the liberal application of cow manure. Writers on "low-tech" agriculture (not to mention any farmers of the old school) generally say that if cow manure is used on a hectare of farmland, at least 100 tonnes are necessary for the first year of crop production. After that about 20 tonnes per year might be adequate. However, cows take up land: one cow requires over a hectare in pasturage, and that is in addition to the hay, grain, and other foods that the animal is given (Lappé, 1991). The "organic" gardener also conveniently ignores the fact that the grass that feeds the cows is probably produced with synthetic fertilizer, which will be in short supply.

The use of cows to keep a garden in production would multiply the necessary land area enormously. There would also be no mechanized equipment to deliver the manure. The knowledge of animal husbandry, under primitive conditions, could certainly not be learned overnight. But I can say from experience that reality hits when the sun is going down and the shovel is getting heavy: shovelling manure shows us that farming is not always easy.

Many of the false figures that appear in discussions of the future are the result of armchair gardening of the worst sort. Growing a tiny patch of lettuce and tomatoes is not subsistence gardening. To support human life, one must be growing grains and similar crops high in carbohydrates and protein, and these foods must be in quantities large enough to supply three full meals a day, every day, for every person in the household. We must also consider that in chaotic times it will certainly not be possible to stroll over to the tap and use a hose to pour unlimited amounts of water over one's plants; on a large garden, the water is whatever the sky decides to send.

There may be an odd solution or two. There are parts of the Earth where population is actually decreasing in absolute numbers, as people mistakenly come to believe that country living is too hard. Well, yes, being squeezed out by multinationals is definitely too hard. But I'm talking about subsistence agriculture, not trying to survive by picking beans for a dollar an hour.

We should not totally discount the practicality of animal husbandry. There are many parts of the world that are not suitable for agriculture, but the same land might produce wild grasses or other vegetation that in turn could feed domesticated animals. Under primitive conditions the density of human population in such areas would have to be very low, and the danger of overgrazing would always be there, but the truth is that there are large parts of the world that supported a pastoral life for centuries.

The only solution that will last a million years, of course, is a return to foraging, and that will especially be true for those who choose to live in that non-arable 90 percent. Hunting and fishing have become unfashionable hobbies, but for the physically fit these skills could be a lifesaver in the next few decades.

22
The Struggle for Localization

The localized economy is probably one of the few self-evident solutions for the future, which otherwise seems to have a rather slim number of options. The question is whether such localization can survive our political leadership. The illegalities of the "localized" life begin with the fact that many of the changes that need to be made to house design, in our post-nearly-all-materials world, are in fact illegal, if not strictly criminal. Here in Canada, one cannot legally build or inhabit a house that does not have conventional plumbing and electricity, for example. And the insurance companies have their say: a house might not be insured if it is heated mainly by wood, because wood is considered a fire hazard. To be respectable, one must use our declining fossil fuels, it seems. In fact, insurance companies now look for all sorts of certification, most of which cannot be considered related to alternative approaches, but all of which are expensive.

The same problem of illegality applies to many other activities, even if these are just common sense. Localized agriculture, as I learned first-hand a few years ago in Ontario, is increasingly plagued by pointless rules related to processing, packaging, labelling, and similar issues, to the extent that small-scale farmers are simply forced out of business. Much of this is done in the name of "health," but such farmers do not have the ability to set up the required laboratories and other equipment that would make their businesses compliant with these ever-expanding regulations.

I'm sure farmers' markets are dismally inefficient at times, lacking the economy of scale that makes the supermarket chains such a delight for the average consumer. But a truck driver here in Canada once pointed out to me that the cost of sending those large vehicles back and forth from Ontario to California or Florida is just not going be feasible as time goes by: for each truck, every trip costs hundreds of dollars.

Even living off the land is largely a criminalized activity, and "protecting the wilderness" does not have a great deal to do with it. Hunting and fishing rules are so designed that, with the exception of Native people, the only people who can engage in these activities are those who are rich enough not to need the food that is thereby supplied. The rules could easily be modified to suit those who are genuinely dependent on the food, but such modifications are rare. Why should a Newfoundlander be arrested for shooting an occasional caribou to feed his family, when a wealthy "sports" hunter can come from outside and take that same animal?

If there is any pattern to all these restrictions, it is that money is constantly directed away from the individual and into the faceless companies, institutions, and government departments that now dominate our lives. If Daniel Boone were alive today, he would be spending his years drifting from one form of incarceration to another.

So, yes, it's true that the localized economy is one of the more practical alternatives to the economic problems that politicians are now stumbling through. But I still think I should get a 10-percent discount on every socially aware book I buy, since I never read that last chapter, "What We Must Do." The key sentence is inevitably, "We must encourage our political leaders to . . . ." Unfortunately our political leaders do not respond positively to those who do such "encouraging." If anything, they are more inclined to lock up such people.

23
Toward a New Medical Science

In a world of increasing population and decreasing resources, medicine in its present form is likely to become
a huge anachronism. As is commonly said, it's often the
case that a doctor, instead of doing something useful such
as diagnosing and treating an ailment, merely signs a pre-
scription. The "in" joke, of course, is that the doctor is the
only one who can afford to buy the pills. And he's not
going to prescribe anything that a cute pharmaceutical representative hasn't been dropping on his desk. But there are
countries that already do better at medicine than the US
and Canada. Thailand, for example, is famous for its excellent—and relatively inexpensive—medical care, and I
was very impressed by what I saw of it in Bangkok. It
seemed as though the largest group of surgery patients was
from Japan; apparently the surgery is cheaper in Bangkok
in spite of the costs of travel and accommodation.

Medicine will have to become less sophisticated.
When I once mentioned half-jokingly to a physician
friend that in the future I'd be willing to carve a set of
crutches for someone with a broken leg, he told me that
I could be charged with practicing medicine without a licence. Yes, I imagine that's true. However, it seems to
me that in the coming systemic collapse, doctors of the

present sort might become rather scarce. In countries with "socialist" medicine, such as Canada, the government funding simply won't be available. And I wonder how many doctors living at the high end of the income scale will make it into the world of "sleeping rough," and would rather perish in suburbia than survive in a ditch. As someone once said, the poorest people of the world won't have to "adjust" to the post-oil world; they've been living there all along.

The sort of medicine that will be practised will be more akin to either first aid or "wilderness medicine." In particular, it will require the kind of doctor who can sometimes work with little or nothing in the way of ready-made instrumentation or medications. (I've been told that it might be possible to store antibiotics—e.g., amoxicillin and cephalexin—for years, if one could keep them cool and dark. But how common are such caches likely to be? And what do we do after that?) Those who will have the necessary skills are likely to have acquired them outside a medical school, and I doubt that the patients will waste time looking for framed diplomas. For self-taught doctors, the home edition of the *Merck Manual of Medical Information* (Beers, 2003) is probably the best book to keep close at hand.

Without high-tech instruments and medication, administering medical aid can be marvellously simple. Instead of spending years learning to identify and treat the various forms of sickness caused by the many viruses, bacteria, and other micro-organisms, for example, all one has to know is that they all look roughly the same:

headaches, fever, diarrhea, nausea, and fatigue. And they all have the same treatment: isolation, rest, warmth, liquids, and nutrients.

I personally have a fondness for primitive medicine, and for years I've been practising "illegal" medicine, usually with myself as my only patient. But I'm aware of both the possibilities and the limitations. Willow bark and wintergreen (*Gaultheria procumbens*), for example, both contain salicylates related to commercial Aspirin. On the other hand, most books on herbal medicine are largely superstitious nonsense, because most such herbs have no medicinal value; Buchman's *Herbal Medicine* (1996) seems one of the best.

We need to know the genuine extent of "primitive" medicine. Some of the Native Americans, particularly the Ojibwa, even practised surgery to a limited extent, but I would think that's pushing the limits. One of the main lessons we'll all learn is that almost any medical problem will either go away or kill you—in either case, there will be nothing further to worry about. Seriously though, most problems do go away, as anyone stuck for years in an "undeveloped" country will attest. The other lesson will be that of the value of physical fitness: in any reasonably wealthy country, there really is no excuse, even at the present time, for a lack of proper diet and exercise; walking doesn't cost a penny.

Where I tend to be somewhat disloyal to the cause of primitive techniques is in what might be called "deep medicine." Over the centuries, medical science has found more and more complexity to the human body. I wouldn't try tampering with hormones for the same reason I wouldn't try replacing the automatic transmission on a car—I just don't have the capacity to do it. A new form of medicine does need to arise, but it must get rid of the "outsider" mentality and create a genuine science for the coming hard times.

24
Where to Live

As various parts of the world collapse, one big question is, "Should I start packing my bags?" There is probably no perfectly rational way for choosing a place to live. Nevertheless, if we are brave enough, or if we have already done some travelling, the factors listed below may be those we want to consider. Unfortunately the travel brochures and retirement advertising give an impression of the "tropical paradise" that is not always realistic, and we must therefore also look at this matter further on—the ideal country might not be what we first imagine.

By far the largest issue is that of time frame. The systemic collapse of modern civilization will consist, as I have said, of two distinct phases, and the border between the two will be marked by the disappearance of money as a means of exchange. Each phase will entail separate considerations.

During Phase One, governments, law, and money will still exist in roughly their present forms, and these will be some of the matters to consider in choosing a place to live. What I am listing below as the issues of economic stability—cost of living and average income—are therefore relevant to Phase One. Even during that first period, however, the longer-term issues of arable land, climate, and family and friends will be very important.

Phase Two will be that in which societal collapse has advanced further. At that point it is unlikely that people will be concerned about the finer points of pension schemes or tax shelters. The list of qualities to consider in a place to live will then be much shorter, and the trivial will be discarded.

We should remember that the readily available information on other countries is mainly geared to tourists, but what such people experience on a 10-day package tour bears little resemblance to long-term residence in a country. Most tourists live in a silly and artificial world, and their lives are not entwined with those of the local people. In fact, tourists are often hated because they regard other countries as their personal playground, and the citizens of that country as their servants.

The tropical paradise can be deceptive. Thailand, for example, has positive and negative aspects. Perhaps in the more rural areas of that country it would be possible to live fairly cheaply. Public transport is usually available, at least for now, so a car might not be necessary. There would be no need for heating fuel or firewood in winter. Food would be cheap and good. But Thailand in general can be quite unpleasant because of its heat, and to some extent because of problems with noise, with environmental destruction, and with overpopulation.

The issue of overcrowding, in Thailand and elsewhere, must also be considered in terms of other issues of societal collapse. If, in the future, the world economy has a crisis that is much worse than the one that started in 2007, I think I would want to be living in a country that has a good deal of uninhabited and undeveloped land where I could be somewhat independent of a money-based economy. In plain English, wherever I live I want to be able to head for the hills. For the same reason, I have no intention of living in a city.

One thing is certain: without motorized transportation, the crowding in the world's cities will ensure that they eventually become death traps. Modern business methods only intensify the weakness: while business-management experts take pride in the cost-effectiveness of "just in time" inventory, they ignore the fact that "just in time" is only a step away from "just out of time." During the Second World War, Leningrad turned to cannibalism when the city was besieged by the Germans (Salisbury, 2003), and such events were far more common in ancient times.

More important than population density in the absolute sense is the ratio of population to the amount of land that can be used to produce crops. Eventually most people will be producing their own food, or at least relying on food grown nearby. A society based mainly on primitive subsistence farming (survival gardening) can have, at the very most, no more than 9 people per hectare of arable land (i.e., 900 people per km^2), and many countries are already well over that density; a more realistic ratio would be 400 people per km^2. A major question therefore is: which countries have a fair amount of arable land?

The following 30 countries (in rank order) have the best ratios: Australia, Kazakhstan, Canada, Niger, Russia, Lithuania, Latvia, Ukraine, Argentina, Guyana, the US, Belarus, Hungary, Zambia, Paraguay, Bulgaria, the Central African Republic, Togo, Turkmenistan, Sudan, Moldova, Finland, Romania, Denmark, Estonia, Mongolia, Namibia, Uruguay, Mali, and Chad. Roughly speaking, the worst areas for this ratio are the Middle East, most of southern and eastern Asia, the islands of the Pacific, and Western Europe (CIA, 2010).

In terms of agriculture, there are also related factors to consider, such as temperature, precipitation, and soil degradation. Of the 30 countries listed above, Kazakhstan, Mongolia, Namibia, Mali, and Chad are quite dry. Most of Central and Eastern Europe have serious problems of soil degradation, but these areas should not necessarily be discounted. Partly because of emigration, they have shrinking populations, for example, and that will be an advantage to those who remain (Bot et al., 2000).

One might be tempted to suggest a sour-grapes theory of the population-to-arable ratio: one could argue that countries with better ratios are merely indicating poor living conditions of some other sort, such as bad politics or economic troubles. To a large extent this is true, but there are important exceptions. The UK and the Republic of Ireland, for example, are very similar in geographic respects, but the UK has three times the population-to-arable ratio; from the standpoint of subsistence farming, the Republic of Ireland would be a far more habitable country.

From my own point of view, good-quality arable land is the most important consideration, either for the sake of growing one's own food, or at least for being close to an area where food is produced and distributed. Political matters are perhaps in second place, while everything else would be far down the list. Nevertheless, I can see how other people would have other priorities.

To some extent the choice of climate is rather a personal matter, depending on what one is used to. Extremes of climate, however, mean that life could become uncomfortable without our accustomed access to central heating or air conditioning. One would ideally be living about halfway between the equator and the poles, but the catch is that many other people have already had the same idea.

Economic stability depends on a number of diverse factors. Countries that rely heavily on exports can be quickly damaged by changes in the world market. A small country is generally in trouble if its income is based on a narrow range of goods or services. Excessive private and public borrowing often leads to debts that cannot be paid. Monoculture and foreign ownership have ruined many countries, even if the facts are rarely printed in newspapers. Modern economics is a complex subject, and when disaster occurs, it seems that no one even knows who to blame.

The cost of living in a foreign country is obviously important, especially for people who hope to have jobs there, but also if they have fixed incomes, or just fixed savings. The odd thing, though, is that the cost of living doesn't really vary all that much from one country to another, contrary to popular belief. A hamburger is always a hamburger, it seems. The cost of living in Moscow is three times as high as in Asunción, Paraguay, but generally the cost of an item in one country will be about the same as its cost in another country (Mercer Human Resource Consulting, 2006). Life out in the countryside may be cheaper, but not greatly, and only relatively: there are no more rural paradises where goods and services can be bought for pennies. More important than the immediate cost of living, of course, is the country's rate of price inflation, which can easily make a dent in income or savings, particularly as the entire world shifts into what I have been calling the economic post-peak Phase One, which is characterized by "stagflation": stagnant wages combined with price inflation. In any case, the best way of dealing with the cost of living in any country is, quite simply, to reduce one's dependence on money by learning to grow food and do carpentry and so on.

Average income (commonly expressed as GDP/capita) is a serious issue for anyone planning to get a job in a distant country and expecting to be paid a local salary. Average income is also a consideration for anyone planning to hire local workers. However, any figure for average income is meaningless unless it is correlated with cost of living, and if both are defined in terms of international dollars or some other universal frame of reference. Making sense of such figures is not always easy. On top of all that, the focus on GDP/capita falsely implies that societies without a money economy are necessarily poor, whereas abundant food and water, for example, are themselves a form of wealth.

There is not a great deal of correlation between a country's cost of living and its average income. There is, however, some tendency for countries with high costs of living to have incomes that are even more unusually high. In a poor country such as Malawi, for example, both the cost of living and the average income are low; in Luxembourg, on the other hand, while the cost of living is somewhat high, the average income is quite remarkable. One reason why people like to move to the US is that the fairly high cost of living is offset by the very high average income. Most countries in Europe, on the other hand, present a bad combination of both high cost of living and low average income.

For those dreaming of escape to distant places, the unfortunate irony is that cheap property and high crime rates often go together. That's true street-by-street, but also country-by-country. It's hard to beat the odds on that one, but perhaps it can be done. And by high crime rates I don't necessarily mean organized crime. A more common question may be the far more subtle issue of whether one will have as neighbours a group of people who persist in minor acts of theft and similar infractions—what is euphemistically referred to as "having an uneasy relationship with the law." Even borderline illegalities can ultimately become heartbreaking for the victims.

There are many countries where the concept of civil liberty is completely absent. In fact, there are many other big political issues that should be considered: political equality, democracy, the whole concept of "the open society." One should not underestimate the pleasures of living in a country with a relatively sane form of government . . . at least for as long as governments last.

Political corruption is a situation in which every day is pervaded by the question of who you know. Although there may be laws and regulations, from the federal to the institutional level, the actual decisions get made, sometimes in secret, on the basis of who has informal power over whom. Daily life is controlled by "families" and petty "mafias," without the guns and glamour of their Hollywood counterparts. There are many forms of corruption, including cronyism (favouritism toward friends), nepotism (favouritism toward family members), bribery, embezzlement, graft, influence peddling, patronage (not always illicit), kickbacks, and electoral fraud. To a large extent corruption is correlated—both as cause and as effect—with poverty, illiteracy, lack of democracy, and lack of freedom of speech and of the press. From the point of view of retirement, perhaps the biggest question about a corrupt country is: what will happen to your bank account after the next palace revolution?

Many countries have laws stating that foreigners cannot retire there permanently unless they offer proof of a guaranteed monthly income, a lump-sum deposit, or an investment of some sort. Having family members already living in the country is an advantage. For those who intend to keep working for a living, having a high-demand profession can make a big difference. Sometimes such laws are rather vague and open to varying interpretation, and getting an application processed may be complicated, time-consuming, and expensive. Within the European Union, it's generally easy for citizens of one country to move to another, but the even there the rules are somewhat variable and subject to change.

There are certainly exceptions, but in general it might be said that immigration laws are getting tighter these days. It's no longer a case of picking a place on a map and packing a suitcase. Most governments are realizing that immigration is often not beneficial to a country. There are far too many people in the world, and most of the blank spaces on the map are not really habitable.

Learning another country's language does not require mental ability, only opportunity (e.g., living there) and determination. Making an effort to learn some of the local language is a good way to make life in a new country more comfortable. Learning a few words of a language, in fact, is one of the principal means of becoming accepted in any society. But obviously the language of the country, or (on the other hand) the likelihood of encountering people who speak one's own language, will have many effects on one's daily life.

Determined loners may be exceptions, but most people would want to consider the choices or necessities of any family members or close friends. If these people are also willing to move, so much the better. If they cannot or will not move, then one's own choices may be restricted. In any case, it may simply be safer to stay in the old, familiar locality, living next to people one has known for years. Even if they are not perfect, it is at least possible to have an idea of what can be can expected from them, whereas strangers in a distant land may offer too many unpleasant surprises.

Ultimately it may be impossible to give up one's present social network. Homesickness can be truly crippling, although those who have previously led a nomadic life may have developed emotional strengths. The move itself can be painful. Besides the emotional strain of travelling to a distant land, there is the problem of selling most of one's possessions before moving to another country, and then buying replacement possessions upon arrival—and perhaps giving up two years later and moving back home again. Sometimes a little perseverance can solve or prevent such problems.

In poorer countries, attempting to copy the way of life of the natives is not a good idea. For example, it is commonly said that a westerner cannot really live comfortably in Thailand for less than about $10,000 a year, and that's the minimum. Most native workers there, on the other hand, live on about $2,000 a year. What it amounts to is that westerners in Thailand would go mad if they tried to live the arduous life that is lived by most natives. Native life in modern times is really just manual labour at starvation wages. If a foreigner moves to a "tropical paradise" at 60 years of age, to go native that person would have to start by being dead for the previous 20 years because the native would be dead by age 40.

I would say, also, that if it costs $10,000 to live in Thailand, then I would rather live in a modern Western country such as Canada, which would probably cost about $15,000 for the same standard of living, but without the disadvantages. In general I have many doubts about putting on shorts and sandals and moving to tropical paradises. I'm sure there are westerners who find such countries pleasant, but my own preference would be for open spaces and a more-northern climate.

There really is no simple answer to the question of where to live. We must each weigh all of the factors, but the measurements themselves can become a personal or intuitive matter. We always look for evidence that the best country is the one in which we were born. Thoreau said, "Though all the fates should prove unkind, / Leave not your native land behind." My own home, Canada, is not entirely native to me; I didn't choose it until age 16, after living in Germany, the UK, and the US. But after so many years in Canada, I will always look for reasons for keeping it as my base of operations. That does not mean it is not a land that can be both geographically and economically trying. Similar paradoxes are true for everyone else in every other country.

We should not lightly dismiss the importance of the emotional ties to our native land, even if we have been "native" to such a land for only a few years. In any case, such ties are not entirely irrational. Our reasons for putting down roots in a particular country may be somewhat accidental, but if we examine ourselves more closely, we may find that when we have stopped our youthful wanderings there is a curious match between personality and landscape.

We must nevertheless remember that the reluctance to leave can be fatal. History is filled with stories of people who failed to heed warnings. The usual cry is, "It can't happen here. This is a civilized country."

25
An Experiment in Country Living

One thing my wife and I learned from nine years in rural Ontario is that country living did not mean freedom from money issues. Of all our expenses, the greatest and most persistent was the car. People who live in the country nowadays are actually more hooked on automobiles than those who live in the city, since there are long kilometres of highway between one's home and other destinations such as shops or a job. For the truly poor, one of the biggest problems in the countryside is that they may have no means of getting to a job even if it is offered to them. For everyone, the obvious alternative to the automobile would be horses, especially as oil becomes scarcer, but unfortunately our highways are not well-designed or regulated for motorists to share the road with horse owners.

Besides the car, our big costs were property taxes and house renovations. We also spent a good deal for food, which is odd in view of the fact that we had a half-hectare market garden and later had many chickens. It was a good thing we had paid cash for the house and land, and for the car, because if we had been paying off debts, we would really have had trouble making ends meet. We were also not as frugal as we might have been. We had a fair amount of money at first because we had sold our house in Toronto, but because we had so much money, we spent it too freely.

Finding a source of income in the country was far harder than in the city. As time went by, we began to realize that there were not many people there who had jobs in the ordinary sense of the word. Most of the people we met were living either on pensions or on welfare, or something similar. The pensioners were sometimes elderly poor people living on nothing but payments from the government. There were only a few people living on company pensions, which provided a higher standard of living. One group of people who had a reasonable income were the few tradespeople that the area could support—carpenters, plumbers, mechanics, and so on. The other large segment of the population was the cottagers, the Torontonians, who were likely to show up only in the summer. These people didn't have to deal with the problem of earning a local income, and some of these even tended to regard the countryside as their personal Disneyland. Most of the local people under retirement age, however, were barely surviving, partly because the entire area pretty well closed down during the winter. The main industry was "tourism," which is sometimes little more than a euphemism for "poverty."

After we bought the property, we seemed to find more and more work that needed to be done to make the place livable, and most of it had to be done before the approach of the first winter. We knew very little ourselves about renovations, and at the same time, we had very few names to work with, so we ended up hiring people without getting multiple estimates for the work to be done. As a result, we were sometimes charged too much money, but we were unable to realize that fact until much later. I would even say that some of those "renovations" should have been left undone. For example, we spent a good deal of money for eavestroughs to be installed around the metal roof of our mobile home, not realizing that a slippery metal roof would result in avalanches of melting snow in the spring, and that those avalanches would simply tear the eavestroughs away.

Many people who live in the country are somewhat ignorant of the arts and sciences, but at the same time they're quite proud of knowing so little. When necessary, they "prove" their own cleverness by avoiding all subjects about which they know nothing. I found myself in a perpetual quandary when talking to locals. Is it better to smile and nod when they talk about "planting by the moon," for example, or is it better just to avoid the company of such people? Either choice can be difficult, since there is no way of removing the sense of alienation, the realization that there are problems of communication.

It's also just not true that all country people are kind-hearted and honest. They are not always willing to welcome city folk with open arms, although that may be partly because the land has only so much capacity for supporting anyone who lives there. There are even some who assume that "city folk" are all rich and lazy and that they deserve to be robbed.

Most country people nowadays know very little about traditional skills. For example, what my wife and I learned over those years about vegetable gardening came almost entirely from books we had read, and from our own experiments. Local people seemed to have little knowledge of such matters as planting times, about soil quality, or about the best crops to plant. The probable reason for this is simply that most country people now buy their food from supermarkets.

Even when those who dwell in the countryside have traditional skills, they are often unwilling to share them. I had really been hoping to learn more about hunting, for example, but I realized (as I had suspected before) that hunting is very territorial. There are only so many deer or moose, and only so many good hunting areas. Hunters usually travel with partners they have known for years, and they are unlikely to reduce their own prospects by giving away their hard-earned knowledge. This "territoriality" is never openly admitted, and has no basis in law except on private land, but it is quite real.

My comments to local people about the joys of rural living sometimes got me some strange looks. The young disliked country living and were rather ashamed of it. The middle-aged took the attitude, not that "anything worth doing is worth doing well," but that it is worth doing only with heavy machinery. I remember seeing two brand-new double-cab pickup trucks going down the road one day with a grand total of four people, merely to eat at a local restaurant—not a big crime, just a vignette. The most knowledgeable people were in their eighties, but the following generations wanted to be part of what they considered the modern world: they were willing slaves to the urban economy that was slowly killing them.

On the positive side, we gradually learned many things about house repair and renovation. In particular we learned how to do a number of carpentry tasks. I even did a bit of plumbing, at least to the extent of replacing old faucets. Electricity, however, remained for me a rather esoteric subject, probably because I found it both dangerous and expensive. Electricity was also unreliable, and violent summer storms would often mean looking for candles and matches.

We learned a great deal about heating with wood. We not only managed to operate a wood stove properly, but we eventually went through the entire process of cutting down trees, sawing them into lengths, splitting the pieces, stacking and storing them, and so on. I became quite adept at using a chainsaw, and I found that using such a machine on a long-term basis requires a good knowledge of maintenance, including sharpening the chain, cleaning the entire machine, and recognizing common problems.

As a long-term "survival skill," operating a chainsaw is rather dubious, of course. How will people operate such things as the world's petroleum runs out? Oil production in 2030 will be less than half that of the year 2000. In any case, according to at least one expert on the subject, if you calculate the money required to operate a chainsaw, and the time involved in maintaining the equipment, you may find that you're better off using a simple bowsaw.

I think using a bowsaw to put together a winter's supply of firewood might require a fair amount of labour, but there may be some sense to the theory. Certainly modern bowsaws are quite good. The blades are of hardened steel, which means they cannot be resharpened and must be discarded eventually, but they last a long time, and buying a lifetime's supply of such blades would be easy enough.

I even bought some antique timber saws, those gigantic devices, often well over a metre long, that our ancestors used for dealing with logs. I learned how to set the teeth (bend them to certain angles) using tools that I had made myself, and how to sharpen them properly. I soon concluded, though, that I didn't have the "ancestral" muscles for such saws. Part of the problem, however, may have been that even after I had done my best to polish the steel surfaces, they were not really smooth, since rust had caused pitting. Much later I discovered that such timber saws can be bought brand new, and that a new timber saw will cut firewood more quickly than a bowsaw.

We learned that there are many other ways of dealing with firewood and heating problems. A smaller house needs less firewood, and so does one with fewer and smaller windows. Good insulation is an enormous help. Another trick from the old days is to use less firewood by sealing off unnecessary rooms in winter. For similar reasons, the stove must be located in the room that will be used the most in the daytime.

We learned many things about vegetable gardening that we didn't know before: the importance of starting with good soil (which we, unfortunately, didn't have), and the importance of keeping an eye on dates and on weather. We learned to identify and defeat many species of harmful insects. We also tried a great many crops and developed a good idea of what crops worked in that area and what ones didn't.

We gained a good knowledge of grains. Corn (maize) is by far the best grain to grow, since the yield per unit of land is quite high, and it requires very little in terms of equipment for growing, for harvesting, or for processing. By "corn," however, I mean the older varieties once grown by the Native people, not modern corn, which is susceptible to insects and diseases. The other grain that did well was rye, mainly because of the sandy soil.

Acquiring chickens was educational in many ways, but by putting up two coops I learned something about the construction of buildings with frames made of two-by-fours, and as part of my learning experience I did everything with non-electric tools except for the somewhat tedious task of cutting chipboard.

I built the first chicken coop with a hand-poured concrete-slab foundation, and a "shed" roof (i.e., one slope rather than two), and the outside of the walls was made of board and batten (vertical boards, with the intervening gaps covered by thin strips). The roof was covered with roll roofing.

For the second coop, I deliberately used entirely different methods, partly so that I could gain further experience. The foundation was of concrete piers rather than a solid slab, the roof had two slopes (and hence two gables), and the outside of the walls was covered with chipboard, which in turn was covered with vinyl siding; all of it admittedly was not so much "traditional" as "transitional." The roof was covered with the same material as the first coop, but in the form of shingles rather than rolls. For the most part, I preferred what I did on the second coop, although I would now say concrete piers are very difficult to build and position neatly without preformed molds and premixed concrete.

Perhaps above all, we learned that it is possible to live with some independence from modern civilization. On those two hectares that were ours by law, but in reality belonged more to Nature, the seasons followed one another, even if we were often too busy to notice. In spring the river roared and bellowed and foamed along its banks, and in winter that same river was a study in black and white. One day the cars will be gone, and so will the money economy. In some ways, the post-industrial world may be quite pleasant.

26
Houses in the Post-Peak World

What are some practical responses to the question of house building in a world where petroleum and other natural resources decline to a small fraction of their present annual production? In particular, let us consider dwellings for a cold climate, where the challenge of adequate housing is greater. One's first thought might seem a simple one: the log cabin. The more we examine the concept, though, the less simple it becomes. If we look closely at today's log cabins—and log houses—the less they seem to serve their original purpose, which was to act as durable warm domiciles requiring only simple tools and taking materials mainly from the surrounding area.

Modern log houses often use logs so big that they can be lifted into place only with heavy machinery, which requires fossil fuels, and so the "pre-industrial" point of it all has disappeared. Most of the cutting and shaping is done with chainsaws, again defeating the purpose. The list of the "inauthentic" goes on: plywood flooring and roofing materials, prefabricated windows and doors, synthetic preservatives. Even the making and use of axes in the future will require a knowledge of metallurgy, but let us assume that this is possible.

For that matter, a modern log house uses far more wood than an ordinary frame house, i.e., a typical suburban house, so there is really no point in putting up a log dwelling when there is machinery for construction available—and especially if, at the same time, the structure is being erected on a well-built road where modern materials could easily be delivered.

We might look back into the log cabins of the eighteenth and nineteenth century in North America. These seem closer to structures that fit the above description of the purpose. But some of these structures are rather daunting, requiring a good deal of both labour and expertise. For example, many houses in those days had hewn logs (logs cut with a special type of axe so that they became squared). The making of cedar shingles for the roof is also not a task for the beginner.

Looking at the wooden houses of the Vikings, or of late Anglo-Saxon England, does not get us much further, because many of these involved woodworking techniques that would probably defeat all but the best of modern woodworkers. Contrary to popular belief, these were not the houses of "primitive" cultures.

Hence we must go even further back in history, to the Iron Age, which in Northern Europe extended from about 500 BCE to about 1000 CE, although there is not much agreement on these dates or the definitions. To a large extent the term "Iron Age" overlaps with that of the "Middle Ages."

There was considerable variety in the forms of Iron Age houses. It was once believed that most of those in

Britain were round, although Geoff Carter (2009, January 15) now questions this. Certainly in Continental Europe, a house was more commonly a large rectangular "hall," or at least the "hall" part of the house was a large rectangular room.

It is important to note that, unlike structures of later times, Iron Age houses had earthen floors, and the main vertical timbers were earthfast, i.e., set directly into the ground and perhaps charred to prevent decay, whereas later buildings had their posts placed on sill beams, which in turn had stone footings. The earlier, earthfast posts would of course still be subject to rotting and might only last a few decades. But raised sills would entail the use of a complete wooden floor, set above the ground, a far more complex design problem.

The walls of Iron Age houses were built of logs, wattle and daub, turf, stone, or a combination thereof, depending on what materials were locally abundant. Both squared and non-squared timbers were used at times. Roofing was probably turf (perhaps with an underlayer of birch bark) or thatch, to judge from more recent forms (Phleps, 1989). The sleeping area might consist of fixed benches running along the sides of the hall.

The fire was just an open area in the middle of the floor, although sometimes with either a sunken or a raised hearth, and the smoke escaped through a hole in the peak of the roof or perhaps the gables, or simply through the thatch. Such a central fireplace may have resulted in a smoky interior on days when a strong wind blew the smoke back into the house, but in general the centrality of the fireplace actually resulted in better radiation of the heat than in later houses, which had enclosed fireplaces built into a wall.

The interiors seem not to have changed much from the early Iron Age to the end of the Middle Ages. Anyone who has read *Beowulf*, a poem originally composed in about the eighth century CE, will recognize many of these features: the large multi-purpose hall, the sleeping benches along the sides, the central fireplace. Even the dwellings of the later Middle Ages, although more sophisticated in the structure of the walls and roofs, often had such a large "communal-style" interior, since not only kings but also farmers tended to live among close-knit groups of people.

27
Survival Gardening

Most people in modern industrial society get their food mainly from supermarkets. As a result of declining hydro-carbon resources, such food will not always be available. Partly as a further consequence of declining hydrocarbons, electricity and metals will also be in short supply. The present world population is enormous, but food supplies per capita have been shrinking for years. In terms of daily life, the most important effect of oil depletion will be that shortage of food. Agriculture will have to become more localized, and it will be necessary to reconsider less-advanced forms of technology that might be called "survival gardening." The following notes are based on a North American perspective, in particular my own experience in farming, but they can be applied more generally to conditions in other parts of the world.

Survival gardening might be defined as having three characteristics. In the first place, as much as possible it involves less-advanced technology; reliance on machinery and chemicals will not be possible without a global economic network to support them, whereas a shovel, a hoe, and a wheelbarrow (with a non-pneumatic tire!) are probably a once-only purchase—and the day will come when even some of these things will not be available.

Eventually horses and other draft animals will be a common sight, although it will take a good many years to breed and train sufficient numbers.

Secondly, survival gardening needs to be water-efficient (Solomon, 1993). Without a municipal water supply or a motorized pump, water for agriculture will no longer be abundant.

Thirdly, survival gardening entails a largely vegetarian way of life. The growing of crops takes less land than raising animals. The production of vegetables is also less complicated than animal husbandry. With a largely vegetarian diet, of course, there can be a danger of deficiencies in vitamins A and B_{12}, iron, calcium, and fat, all of which can be found in animal food.

It is true, however, that some animals can make good use of less-fertile land, and animal manure can be used to supply humus and to recycle whatever essential elements (N, P, K, etc.) are in the soil. Anyone serious about keeping animals for meat may find that chickens are the simplest to deal with. There are also sources of meat other than domesticated animals: fishing, trapping, and hunting would be useful skills.

Besides grains and fruits, the most useful food plants in temperate climates belong to about nine families, including the *Amaryllidaceae* (garlic, leeks, onions), *Chenopodiaceae* (beets, chard), *Brassicaceae* (broccoli, Brussels sprouts, cabbage, collards, kale, kohlrabi, rutabagas, turnips), *Leguminosae* (beans, peanuts, peas), *Umbelliferae* (carrots, parsnips), *Convolvulaceae* (sweet potatoes), *Solanaceae* (peppers, potatoes, tomatoes), and *Cucurbitaceae* (squash).

A good general rule is to choose old-fashioned (including heirloom or heritage) varieties rather than modern, big plants rather than small (but small fruit rather than big), pole or vine rather than bush. Popular varieties over the last several decades, unfortunately, have been heading in the opposite direction. Commercial growers want faster varieties; urban gardeners want small ones. Choosing varieties that are hardy and drought-resistant means going in the opposite direction. The rule does not always work—bush beans are not necessarily worse than pole beans, for example—but it serves as a guide. A somewhat similar guide is to look for something that closely resembles a wild plant, or is roughly the same thing as a wild plant—dandelions, mustard, or purslane, for example.

Modern-day city dwellers who live sedentary lives are likely to focus on low-calorie food. Those concerned about survival gardening will want to do the opposite; country living requires substantial meals. Survival gardening means the production of a large number of kilocalories ("calories") with a small amount of labour and a small amount of risk, and perhaps with not a great deal of land. With these factors in mind, one could say that there are not so many crops worthy of attention. There is no such thing as a perfect type of food to grow, because there are advantages and disadvantages to every type. Reliance on a single crop would be dangerous, and variety is essential. We never know exactly what will happen, and no rules are absolute.

Many of what might seem obvious choices may be

questionable. Potatoes are highly susceptible to Colorado potato beetles, blight, and several other pests and diseases. The brassicas are excellent for vitamins and minerals, but some of them are bothered by pests and diseases; curly kale is perhaps the least trouble-prone.

A good starting point would be to focus on corn (maize), beans, and squash, the main crops grown by the Native peoples of North America. These three crops are easy to grow, and they require little or no watering if the plants are well spaced. Corn and beans, eaten together, provide excellent protein. *Corn* here means non-hybrid field corn (basically, what is known as "Indian corn"), not sweet corn. *Beans* means dry beans, not green beans. *Squash* means winter squash (hard squash, such as butternut and acorn), not summer squash.

In areas where there is sufficient summer heat and sunshine, corn is by far the most important crop to grow. Other grains can be substituted, but these require more tools as well as complicated methods of threshing and winnowing. They also have lower yields per hectare, and the greater amount of land makes a horse and plow almost a necessity if one is expecting to feed an entire family on a largely vegetarian diet. Without mechanization or fertilizer, a hectare of rye, for example, yields about 1,000 kg per year, resulting in only 3 or 4 million calories, barely enough for three or four hard-working people.

Most of the world's land is not suitable for agriculture. Either the soil is not fertile or the climate is too severe. Anyone intending to buy a piece of land should take a sample of the soil and have it tested by a government-approved laboratory, while services of that kind are still available. If the soil is really poor to begin with, and especially if it is very low in potassium or phosphorus, there is not a great deal that can be done about it, at least with the resources available in a survival situation.

Soil used for the growing of crops must have adequate amounts of organic matter (humus), which can come directly from decomposed vegetation or from animal manure. Organic matter holds water and air in the soil, contains—often to a rather limited extent—some of the elements needed for plant growth, and provides an environment for small organisms that are essential to the fertility of the soil.

Farmland must also have adequate amounts of about 16 elements, naturally occurring or otherwise. These are boron, calcium, carbon, chlorine, copper, hydrogen, iron, magnesium, manganese, molybdenum, nitrogen, oxygen, phosphorus, potassium, sulfur, and zinc. Of these 16, the most critical are phosphorus (P), potassium (K), and especially nitrogen (N). Calcium and magnesium are probably next in importance. Some of the elements may be found in organic matter, but the quantities are generally insufficient. These elements might be abundant in the soil before any cultivation is done, but whenever crops are harvested, a certain amount of the three critical elements is removed.

The problem of inadequate amounts of the 16 elements is generally remedied nowadays by adding fertilizer, which can be artificial or can come from such sources as rock dust—the latter a fashionable "soil amendment" that will no longer be available without hydrocarbon-based mining and transportation. Acidity can be counteracted by adding crushed limestone (again, not likely to be available) or wood ashes, which contain calcium. Planting any legume, such as beans or peas, can provide nitrogen, since bacteria in the roots take nitrogen from the air; the plants must be dug back into the soil.

Primitive societies had a simple but imperfect solution to the problem of maintaining fertility: abandonment. No fertilizer was used, except for ashes; as a result, the soil became exhausted after a few years, so the fields were abandoned and new ones were dug.

Nevertheless, a small human population might survive on agriculture, at least if it reverted to some primitive methods. Some Asian cultures brought wild plant material from the mountains and used it as fertilizer, thereby making use of the N-P-K (etc.) of the wilderness. Many other cultures used wood ashes. The nutrient "source" of the wilderness fed the nutrient "sink" of the farmland. (This is one of the basic principles behind all "organic gardening," although few practitioners would admit it or even know it.)

A common response to the N-P-K problem, used in many countries for centuries, has been to turn crop waste into compost and put it back onto the land. The problem with that technique is that one cannot create a perpetual-motion machine. Every time the compost is recycled, a certain amount of N-P-K is lost, mainly in the form of human or animal excrement after the crops are eaten, but also as direct leaching and evaporation. One can come closer to sustainability by recycling those human and animal wastes, but the recycling will always be less than perfect. After all, nitrogen, phosphorus, and potassium are elements, and by definition they cannot be created. Of the three main elements, nitrogen is by far the most subject to loss by leaching, but to some extent that can also happen with phosphorus and potassium.

There are partial solutions that are worth considering. Besides using vegetable compost and animal manure for increasing the sustainability of agricultural land, many societies have employed such related techniques as crop rotation, fallowing (leaving land uncultivated for a year or so), cover cropping (growing plants to protect the soil when not used for crops), and green manuring (growing plants to be dug back into the soil for their nutrients). Such practices also replenish the humus content of the soil. Fallowing and cover-cropping can even partly replenish the important elements: weathering can break rock particles down to release those elements, although this may be a very slow process in cool climates, and plants with deep roots can draw such elements to the surface. Some of these techniques are difficult with hand tools, however. In other countries, especially in Asia, vegetation was brought in from the hills, or mud was taken from streams that ran down from the mountains (King, n.d.).

The term *irrigation* refers to any use of water other than the direct use of rainfall or other natural precipitation. In a post-oil economy it will not be possible to use a motorized water supply for irrigation. Yet if one were to try using an old-fashioned hand pump to get the water out of the well, a good deal of manual labour would be involved. A garden needs about 2 or 3 cm of water a week. On a garden of 1 hectare, that would amount to at least 200 m^3 of water. That would mean carrying a bucket to the pump about 6,700 times a week, except when it rained. Not very practical.

What the North American Native people and pioneers did was to give the plants plenty of space, and then just rely on the rain. Almost any type of crop, given enough room, can be left to the mercy of the weather, although some crops need to be watered as seeds or seedlings. The essence of water-efficient gardening is to space out the plants so that the distance between them is greater than most modern gardening manuals recommend. That way the roots can spread out and explore in all directions to find the water that has been stored there over the previous months. In other words, contrary to popular belief, "intensive gardening" is not practical without a garden hose and an unlimited supply of water. More plants per unit of land simply means using more water per unit of land. With such a method, the lack of bare ground between rows also means that it is not easy to get a hoe to the weeds; as L. H. Bailey said long ago, intensive gardening is just "cultivating the backache" (1910, p. 451).

Growing one's own vegetables is sometimes neither easy (labour-free) nor simple (uncomplicated). It's only easy and simple if the garden is just a suburban backyard, and if a family doesn't have to get through the winter on what it has produced. Even after reading many books on the subject, to be good at growing crops takes years of practice.

For one thing, it may take a while to develop one's body to the point where it can properly handle the necessary walking, digging, and carrying. It also requires understanding the principle that a period of rest can be as important as a period of work. A sense of timing is vital, both short-term and long-term: it's possible to use hand tools to get a large boulder out of the ground, but not if the attempt is made in a mad rush. In order to be able to smile with satisfaction later at one's labours, it is necessary to build up the muscles while maintaining that sense of balance.

The mental ability has its own prerequisites. I have had a fair number of academic pursuits over the years, and I can honestly say that farming ranks quite high as an intellectual challenge. When a crop does well or poorly, there are many reasons why that is so, and anyone who expects to have a sufficient harvest must find those reasons. To be a farmer, one must at the same time be a geologist, a microbiologist, an entomologist, a mammalogist, a botanist, and a meteorologist—among other things. There are dozens of species of insects that can attack the crops, and there are dozens of mammals that can do the same. Every kind of weed has a name and a nature, and one type is not dealt with the same as another. It is necessary to develop an eye for the weather, so that one can look at the sky and see tints and shades that would be invisible to a city dweller. And as with any other serious skill, there is a point at which a highly conscious and overly intellectual comprehension must be replaced or at least supplemented by a subconscious presentiment that might be labelled instinct or intuition.

But the work of gardening is not drudgery. On the contrary, there is nothing like growing one's own food to dispel the problem of what Marx called "alienated labour." Unlike so much of what constitutes urban life, gardening fulfills a primal need. We are at last making the connection between "what we do" and "what we need."

Gardening is also fascinating in terms of the acquisition of knowledge. When we grow our own food, we can learn a great deal, and our curiosity about Nature will always be aroused. So much of that ancient art has been lost, or nearly lost, and whenever we are out in the fields we are reclaiming those skills. Whenever we plant seeds and watch them grow, we are preserving or rediscovering a valuable item of human knowledge. The world will need that wisdom soon enough, because that is the way people used to live, and that is how they will live.

28
Growing Your Own Grains

Most of what are called grains are members of the grass family, which has the scientific name of *Gramineae* or *Poaceae* (Logsdon, 1977). Grains are the most important plants in the human diet, contributing most of the carbohydrates as well as a certain amount of protein, vitamins, minerals, and fibre. Generally speaking, grains are quite undemanding in terms of soil or weather.

Unfortunately most of our knowledge of raising grain in small quantities with simple tools has been lost, or at least it is hard to find. Nearly all of the present-day research is geared to modern agribusiness—hybridization, genetic engineering, and very expensive machinery and chemicals. The information gained from such research will be of no use when there is a breakdown of the technical and economic infrastructure. Grains are all that stand between the human race and starvation, but the human race has made very little effort to record the fundamental information about pre-industrial production.

With the exception of corn (maize), grains might not be a subject for the beginning "survivalist"; to make a significant contribution to your diet, they require a good deal of land. Beyond a certain level of production, also, you need to use draft animals, and that in turn requires learning many other skills. The entire process of using grains, from sowing to bread baking, requires equipment of many sorts, even if you are working at only a "medieval" level. But I know these things are not impossible, because I myself have eaten bread that I baked from grain that I sowed. And even if grain production does not become a significant part of daily life right away, it is important that the knowledge be put to use at least to some extent, and thereby preserved.

For the purposes of survival and small-scale gardening, never get involved with hybrids or with genetically engineered grains; this is most commonly an issue with corn. Hybrid grain cannot reproduce properly, so if you wanted more of the same you would have to buy again from the supplier. Genetically engineered grains pose a number of dangers, but the biggest problem is again that of reproduction, because such grains are often given a "terminator gene" that prevents you from regrowing such seeds. The excuse for creating such a gene is that the manufacturers need to recover the cost of research and development—sounds like science fiction, but it isn't.

Types of Grain

Wheat, barley, rye, and oats are grown in roughly the same way. The main difference is the hardiness of the grain. Wheat requires fairly good soil, and it cannot tolerate far-northern climates, whereas barley is less demanding, and rye will grow on almost any kind of land and in a great range of climates. Corn (maize) is a much larger plant, grown widely spaced, but producing abundantly.

Buckwheat (which is not a true grain, although it is used in the same way) is worth considering, especially for cold climates or poor soil, although a crop is easily destroyed by heavy rain. Proso millet (*Panicum miliaceum*) or sorghum (*Sorghum bicolor*) would be worth growing, especially on very dry land. Only a few types of grain are described below, but actually there are dozens of cultivated species. One of the world's most important grains, of course, is rice, but it's not a very practical crop for most of North America.

Many grains have "spring" and "winter" varieties. Spring varieties are sown in the spring and harvested in the summer. Winter varieties are planted in the fall and left to grow a little. When spring arrives, those winter varieties will start growing again, before spring varieties have a chance to get going. Winter varieties will usually have a higher yield than spring varieties.

Cultivation

In North America, most grains are grown in roughly the same manner. Corn, sorghum, and rice are exceptions. But for wheat, rye, barley, oats, millet, and buckwheat, the "pre-industrial" process is essentially that of digging or plowing the land, and then broadcasting the grain and covering it.

Grain grows best on loose, well-tilled soil. However, you need the grain to be about 2 to 5 cm deep, and the easiest way to achieve this with hand tools is to leave the ground fairly rough and lumpy when you're spading or plowing it. If you were to rake and smooth the soil before sowing the grain, you'd be faced with the problem of burying it. So broadcast the grain on rough ground, and then use a rake to get the grain properly covered.

The oldest and simplest way of sowing grain is broadcasting: every couple of steps, throw out a handful of grain, either to the left or to the right. Don't worry too much about precision, or about the fact that birds and other creatures will come along later to get their percentage. When broadcasting, you should be able to cover a strip about 2 m on each side of you, so to cover the whole field, you'll be walking parallel strips about 4 m apart. When you've sown all the grain, go over it with a rake to cover it.

If you're growing on clay soil, try to get the soil broken up a little more finely, and don't let the grain get so deeply buried. With sandy soil, the opposite is true: you might want to get it down at least 5 cm. An ideal day on which to do your broadcasting would be just before a rain. You should still use a rake to cover the grain, but the rain will do the final smoothing for you and preserve more of the grain from depredation by animals.

Weeds

After you've sown a grain, it's often difficult to do any weeding, so weeds can be a serious problem, especially when you're working with a piece of ground that you have only recently converted from a wild or semi-wild state. Wild land may have many species of weeds that will try to compete with your grain crop. Weeds are a nuisance for several reasons: they will reduce the yield of your grain crop, they will add their own seeds to your harvest, and they could even ruin your stored grain if their leaves start to ferment and heat up. There are basically three solutions to the problem of weeds: intense pre-cultivation, row planting, and planting of another species.

Pre-cultivation involves digging or otherwise tilling the land several times. In early spring, dig the land once and turn up all the weeds so that they die from exposure. About two weeks after you've tilled the field, it will start to look green again as a new crop of weeds comes up. Till the soil again so that the new weeds are killed. If you have the time and energy, do the same thing again after another two weeks. By then, you should have a field sufficiently free of weeds for you to grow a successful crop of grain.

If you know that your land is still going to be producing lots of weeds, you could try growing the grain in rows so that you can walk around the growing plants and use a hoe to get at the weeds.

A third method of dealing with weeds is to start with another crop and crowd out the weeds before they get a chance. You could, for example, plant clover or alfalfa and dig it back into the field before it flowers. Or you could plant buckwheat, which would certainly supply organic matter and provide you with a grain itself.

Harvesting

A few months after it starts growing, your grain is ready to harvest. Hand harvesting tends to shake up the plants more than harvesting by machine, so some of the grain might fall to the ground and be lost. To avoid the problem, the grain should be collected when it is still somewhat chewy, not completely hard. Pick out a few grains from time to time and test them to see what stage they're at. When they're at the correct stage, you'll notice that the entire plant has become a different colour: about half green, half yellow. Another indicator may be the suddenly greater interest taken by the birds.

With primitive farming, the yield will be less than half of that obtained with modern equipment and fertilizer. The yield you are likely to get will be anywhere from 300 to 3,000 kg/ha, depending on the type of grain, the weather, and many other factors. At the low end would be rye, buckwheat, and millet, although these should produce roughly 1,000 kg/ha. Field corn, however, might result in as much as 3,000 kg/ha.

When the grain is ready to be cut, you'll need a good stretch of dry weather. Since it's summertime, you're pretty likely to get good weather, but you can never be certain. Do whatever you can to get the grain harvested on dry days.

Hand harvesting generally means using a sickle. What you have to do is to bend down, grab a handful of grain, and then cut it off by reaching around it with the sickle and cutting it off. There's a lot of bodily movement involved, so go slowly and take lots of breaks, at least until you get used to it.

A sickle is a one-handed tool, whereas a scythe (Tresemer, 1981) is for two hands and allows you to stand up. You can go much faster with a scythe than with a sickle, since you don't have to move around so much. There are two general types of scythe, one with a curved handle and one with a straight one. The type with the curved handle (actually double-reflexed, like an archery bow) is sometimes called "American style," although it appears in several other countries, and the straight-handled type is called "Austrian style," although it's not just Austrian. The Austrian style is not well known in North America, but it's far superior to the American style, since you don't have to bend your back constantly to use it. A lot of modern Austrian-type scythes have aluminum handles, which work quite well.

At this point, however, I should dispel a popular myth. Throughout world history, the scythe alone was almost never used to harvest grain. It was commonly used for cutting hay, but not grain. The problem with a scythe is that, by itself, it cannot lay the stalks straight enough for them to be gathered and bound. The solution, invented mainly in the nineteenth century, was to attach to the scythe a set of long, finger-like projections known as a cradle. It's possible to harvest grain with a scythe that has no cradle, but it does a somewhat messy and wasteful job.

But the scythe with a grain cradle is not necessarily superior to the sickle, and the latter is still used in many countries. Scythes with cradles are heavy, they are dangerous (people sometimes cut their legs while flipping the stalks off the cradle and onto the ground), and they still do a less neat job than sickles, so grain tends to be wasted. A final advantage of a sickle is that you can leave a longer stubble if you wish to do so; those longer stalks can later be dug in to replace some of the organic matter in the soil.

Cutting the grain is the first part of the harvesting process. After that comes gathering and banding. The sheaf (bundle) can be any size, although some people like to have it as big as can be held in two arms. In the old days, the sheaf was held between the legs and tied with a few stalks of the same grain; the stalks were wrapped around the sheaf to act as a band, the two ends of the band were put together and twisted three or four times, and then the twisted part was tucked back under the main part of the band to keep everything together. Nowadays baling twine or something similar, if available, does the job more easily if less cheaply; to keep the stalks parallel in the sheaf, cut the twine long enough so that it can go around the sheaf several times before being knotted.

Set the sheaves upright in groups of about half a dozen, called shocks or stooks. Leave them outside for at least a month to finish ripening. Then put them together in a stack (rick): lay about 30 sheaves together on the ground with their heads inward so that you're forming a tight circle with no space in the middle; lay more sheaves around this to form a wider circle; and then start another layer on top of the first circle. Continue until you've got about a dozen layers, forming a sort of cylindrical tower. Cover it with a tarpaulin if possible.

It's best to keep it outdoors, in the rick, for at least a month before you bring it in, thresh it, and store it. Unthreshed grain will remain in good condition almost indefinitely, as long as it stays dry. In fact, if you thresh and store the grain too early, it will heat up, which means that it will not germinate later when you need it to.

Whenever you're ready to thresh, put the bundles on a clean floor (but not bare concrete, since you'll never get rid of the grit) and beat them with a flail, which is a tool somewhat like a broomstick to which a shorter stick is attached with a leather thong. Or you just can pick up the sheaves and beat them over a horizontal pole, or even over the back of a chair. Actually almost anything can be used to beat the grain, and human or animal feet might do as good a job. All that matters is to get the grain free from the stalks.

The next stage is winnowing, to separate the grain from the chaff—the thin husks or scales that enclose each grain. One way is to wait for a windy day and then pour the grain from one container into a second that is placed somewhat lower. As the grain falls, the chaff is caught by the wind and whisked away. A more laborious method is to use a fan as a substitute for the wind.

Store the grain in any rodent-proof container, but be sure that your crop is quite dry before you do so. If you have any doubts about the dryness, keep it in a shallow pile and stir it frequently to keep the temperature to a minimum. Part of your harvest must be put aside for the next year's planting. Grain that's saved for seed must be kept alive, and that means it should be really dry before it's stored.

The rest of the grain is then ready to be ground into flour. If you wanted to be really old-fashioned, you would use one stone shaped somewhat like a pastry rolling pin, and another much larger, flatter, and perhaps concave stone. Nowadays it might be more practical to use a hand-cranked steel grain mill.

Wheat (*Triticum aestivum* and *T. turgidum*)

Wheat is easy to grow, since it doesn't need rich soil or much rain. It's easy to process, because the grain falls away from the chaff. It's popular as a food because it's high in gluten, which is what makes bread both chewy and light. Overall, wheat is the most nutritious of grains, since it has a fair amount of protein and vitamins.

For wheat to grow well, the soil should not be acidic, wet, or sandy. Wheat requires a long growing period, generally about 150 days, with not too much heat but a good deal of sunlight. The annual rainfall should be between 50 to 100 cm, and there should be a nice dry period during the harvest.

Wheat is subject to a disease called rust; agribusiness solves the problem by constantly creating new cultivars. As a small-scale grower, you are probably hoping to produce your own seed grain perpetually, so rust can be serious, especially in humid southern regions.

Some varieties of wheat are "spring" wheat, planted in spring and harvested in the same summer. Other varieties are "winter" wheat, planted in the fall, left to die down in winter, then harvested in the summer. Winter wheats usually produce higher yields but can sometimes be killed by severe cold.

Both spring and winter wheats can be divided into

"soft" wheats and "hard" wheats, and also into "red" and "white" varieties. All kinds of wheat are interchangeable in cooking, but some kinds are preferred for certain purposes. Hard red winter wheat, used for making bread, is resistant to cold winters. It is commonly grown in the central US. Hard red spring wheat, used for both bread and pasta, is grown in areas that are too cold even for hard red winter wheat: the north-central US and the Canadian prairies. Soft red winter wheat, used for pastry, requires more moisture and cannot tolerate great cold. It is grown in the southeastern US and in the Pacific Northwest. White wheat is not quite so common, but it is found in the Pacific Northwest, in the northeastern US, and in parts of Canada. Durum wheat, used for pasta, is a separate species, *T. turgidum*; because it is the most drought-resistant of all wheats, it is grown in the north-central US and parts of the Canadian prairies.

The best time to plant winter wheat is at the time of the first frost. The planting time is critical, because wheat that has begun stooling (producing stalks) is less resistant to cold weather. In addition, winter wheat should be planted after the danger from an insect pest called Hessian fly. Learn the "fly date" for your area, the date after which the insect is not active; this will be roughly September 15. Spring wheat should be planted fairly early, perhaps three or four weeks before the average date of the last spring frost. If you are broadcasting wheat, use about 1.5 kg per 100 m^2 of land, or about 100 kg/ha.

Rye (*Secale cereale*)

As a "survival" food, rye is an excellent choice. It does very well in cold areas, and it is highly tolerant of poor soil, doing well even on very sandy soil. It is also less bothered by birds than other grains.

Ergot sometimes infects rye. This fungus is easy to identify because it makes the grain black and swollen. Keeping your stored grain dry can help prevent this problem. Sowing seed that's more than a year old may help, since the fungus doesn't stay viable after that length of time. If you get ergot anyway, but you have some salt, you could dump your grain into a mixture of 250 ml (1 cup) of salt to 1 L of water, stir until the infected grain floats to the top, and then dry out the good grain.

Barley (*Hordeum vulgare*)

Like wheat, barley comes in both "winter" and "spring" varieties, but winter types are grown only in the southern US. If you have trouble with deer, you can get a bearded, rough-awned barley that the deer won't touch. Alkaline soil is fine for barley, but not acidic soil, and it does better in clay soil than in sandy soil.

Barley may not be the most practical crop for small-scale gardening because removing the husks really requires a pearling machine or a roller mill. It's possible to put the entire grain through an ordinary hand mill, but only if you like a highly fibrous product. There are hull-less (naked) forms of barley, however, and although their yield is not as great they might be suitable for the small farm.

The growing of barley nevertheless has a number of

advantages. The yield of barley is often better than that of wheat. Barley can stand much colder climates than wheat, and it has a great ability to withstand drought. Barley bread will not rise like wheat bread, but sprouted barley is the main source of malt, used in beer making.

Oats (*Avena sativa* and *A. nuda*)

Oats have wide-spreading branches and flowers that hang down, very much unlike wheat, rye, or barley. There are both "winter" oats and "spring" oats, but winter oats can be grown only in very mild climates. Most modern forms of oats have hulls. Hull-less varieties (*A. nuda*) are available, but they yield less, are more subject to deprivations from birds, and do not resist cold weather as well. Oats do very well in cool weather and should be planted as soon as the ground can be worked. The crop will grow on most types of soil but does best on clay loam.

Proso Millet (*Panicum miliaceum*)

The word *millet* is applied to quite a number of grains. One millet that is worthy of attention is usually called proso millet or broomcorn millet—the latter a misleading term, since brooms are made from sorghum, not millet. It is ready for harvesting three months after planting, much more quickly than wheat. The grain is quite undemanding in terms of soil, moisture, or weather. The shiny hulls are hard to detach from the grain, but there is little need to do so, because the entire grain can be ground to produce a mild-tasting flour.

Sorghum (*Sorghum bicolor*)

Sorghum can withstand considerable drought, although it can't handle cold weather, and it is easy to harvest and process. For planting, you need to wait until about 10 days after the last spring frost date. Sorghum will grow in the same kind of land that will support corn. Plant the grains about 10 cm apart, in rows about 75 cm apart, although in dry regions you'll need to use wider spacing. Then you'll need 100 frost-free days after that for the grain to ripen properly, so it isn't a particularly early crop. You need only about 10 kg of sorghum to plant an entire hectare. The yield is also impressive: about double that of wheat.

Corn (*Zea mays*)

Nowadays there are two main types of corn, sweet corn and field corn, although these are not botanical distinctions. The former is the type that we usually eat as "corn on the cob," while the latter is the type that is either ground into cornmeal or fed to animals. In general, the sweet varieties of corn are less suitable for drying, and they have more problems with diseases and insects. Field corn, on the other hand, is definitely worth growing. It has a higher yield per hectare than any other temperate-climate grain, and (unlike some other grains) there is no complicated threshing or winnowing involved. In Canada, the US, and Europe today, by far the most common type of corn is a field corn called "yellow dent." Less common is "flint" corn, a harder type (hence the name) that lacks the "dent" at the top of the dried kernel. Popcorn, the most ancient of all the surviving types of corn, is actually a sort of flint corn.

In modern times, however, you're unlikely to find varieties of corn that qualify as both "field corn" and "open-pollinated," with the exception of those that are generally known as "Indian" or "ornamental" corn. As long as you don't choose a variety that has too long a growing season for your area, you should do fine. The hard ("flint") types do better in areas where spring or fall frosts may be a danger.

There are no "organic" methods that will totally prevent insects from attacking your corn. There are, however, a few tricks that will reduce insect problems considerably: grow field corn rather than sweet corn; grow open-pollinated types; plant late; bury or burn all crop residues (the plants after the ears have been harvested); grow corn with longer and tighter husks (older varieties are best for this reason); keep your soil in good condition; and don't peel back the tips of the husks to see if the ears are ripe (since that invites insects).

Plant your corn around the time of the last spring frost, but if you want to play it safe, you might want to wait a few more days because corn is sensitive to cold weather. Just make sure you give the plants plenty of room: the kernels should be planted about 2 to 5 cm deep and about 60 cm apart, in rows that are about 1 m apart. In an arid area, you might want to increase these distances. Many of the Native tribes planted the kernels in clusters separated by perhaps 1 m in every direction; this method may have conserved water or ensured that a few plants would survive depredation by animals. If you're growing field corn, you probably don't need to add water, but in an arid climate you may have to give each plant an occasional cup of water during the first weeks of growth.

Each corn plant has a male part and a female part. The male part, at the top of the plant, produces pollen, which is so light that the wind should be able to blow it onto the female part of another plant. That is why corn should be planted in blocks rather than single rows.

In late summer, when the corn begins to ripen, you can pick some of it and eat it as "corn on the cob," just as with sweet corn. To remove an ear, grasp it firmly, then twist it while you bend it downwards. You can leave the husk on and place the ears in the ashes of a fire. Most of the ears, however, should be left until the plants have gone brown and dried. The ears can then be brought inside. Pull the husks back and hang the corn up to dry.

The Native people crushed the kernels into flour in a huge wooden mortar and pestle, or the crushing was done with two stones, the bottom one wide and flat, the top one smaller and rounder. The finished cornmeal was used to make soups, pudding, or bread. Nowadays a good steel hand mill does a quicker job.

Buckwheat (*Fagopyrum esculentum*)

Buckwheat is not a member of the grass family at all, but of the *Polygonaceae*. It can handle the poorest of soils and is often used as a green manure, dug into the soil to improve it. Buckwheat will grow well in hot weather, but it needs cool weather later in order to produce seed; on the other hand, frost can quickly kill buckwheat. Spring planting can be risky if you want grain, because warm weather might arrive too quickly; midsummer is the best time for planting if you want to produce grain. One problem is that the grain doesn't all ripen at once; try to estimate the point of maximum yield. There's no real need to remove the hulls, since they're fairly soft; you can just grind up the entire grain.

29
Putting Meat on the Table

Almost any creature in the animal kingdom can provide food. You can eat most kinds of insects. Other sources of animal food are the many kinds of shellfish. Another important source of animal food, of course, is fish. Reptiles and amphibians can be clubbed or speared. Birds can be caught in snares. Mammals can be killed with weapons of various sorts, but they can also be trapped in deadfalls or snares.

Hunting

A gun or two would be very useful, at least until the world's ammunition runs out. Owning a gun, however, does not mean you can actually hit anything with it, so be sure to do plenty of target practice well before your life depends on being able to shoot accurately.

In a survival situation, you would generally not go hunting in the usual manner of carrying a specific type of gun and looking for a specific type of prey, in accordance with the time of year and particularly in accordance with the type of licence you're carrying. On the contrary, if you were truly living off the land, you would need to be prepared for any sort of wild meat, whether it was frogs or moose.

There's no such thing as a perfect gun, so you have to make your own decisions. Of course, as they say, "First you choose the ammunition. Then you choose the gun to go with it." A .22 rifle is quiet, with very lightweight ammunition; if necessary, even large animals can be killed with such a gun if you fire repeatedly and hit the vital areas. A 12-gauge shotgun is certainly powerful and will take a variety of ammunition, but it's only good for short distances. You could use a shotgun for deer, especially in thick forest where the animal would be sighted at only a short distance. Probably most people would prefer a rifle, a Remington or Winchester in .308 calibre, perhaps mounted with a telescope in the 1.5x–4x range. A lever-action .30/30, however, is light and easy to carry. Bolt (and, to some extent, lever) actions are less trouble-prone than either pump or semi-automatic and might therefore be preferable in a world without easy access to gunsmiths. It's really hard to say, though, what constitutes the one best survival gun. Based on what Native people do, and what military survival experts seem to prefer, it would seem that a single-shot .22 is the best choice, if you intend to have only one gun. On the other hand, in most of North America it is illegal to shoot big game with something as small as .22 ammunition. So as long as governments endure, the .22 is a somewhat theoretical survival weapon.

Buy your gun or guns as soon as possible, and buy as much ammunition as your budget will allow, before it becomes too expensive or too restricted. Unfortunately the laws regarding the possession of guns and ammunition can change in irrational and unpredictable ways over the years. Throughout history, economic collapse has tended to be correlated with repressive legislation, and at the best of times most governments seem uncomfortable with allowing ordinary citizens to hold weapons.

Virtually all North American mammals are suitable as food. Porcupines can be easily clubbed, and hence form a good source of food in emergencies. Deer and moose are common big-game animals, while sheep, elk, and antelope are taken in other areas. In parts of the southwestern US, smaller animals, including mice and pack rats, once provided a large part of the diet. Rabbits can be killed with simple throwing sticks, sometimes after they have been driven into long nets by community drives—long lines of people walking towards the rabbits, driving them towards the nets.

A possible problem with hunting for game in post-collapse times is that there might be far too many people doing it. That's especially likely when many people start to ignore the game laws, and every day is "open season." On the other hand, there are three good reasons, all somewhat interrelated, why there might not be such a problem of excessive hunting. The first is that the shortage of fuel will cut down the number of motorized vehicles—cars, trucks, ATVs, snowmobiles, motorboats—on which the modern hunter depends. The second and related reason is that the average member of modern industrial civilization lacks the physical stamina to go wading through a swamp all day, looking for a moose. A third reason is that there are simply not that many people who have the skills for serious hunting.

Don't laugh at bows and arrows; some of the best hunters use them instead of firearms. Arrows are silent, so you have a better chance at a second shot, and for the same reason you have less worry about human intruders. Unlike rifle cartridges, arrows can be reused easily, and the materials to make new ones are not hard to find. Don't underestimate the killing power of a sharp broadhead.

Trapping

Books on primitive technology often show dozens of types of traps, but in reality you would use only a few (Cooper, 1978; Goodchild, 1999; Nelson, 1973; Wheat, 1967). You would probably want to set a fair number of traps if you expected to get something to eat, but it's unlikely that you would use many types. Most traps fit into two general categories: deadfalls and snares. A deadfall is a log or rock held by a support attached to some sort of trigger mechanism; when the trigger is moved, the support falls, and the log or rock lands on the animal. Usually some sort of bait food is attached to the trigger in order to attract the animal. Snares, on the other hand, sometimes have triggers and bait, but not always, since the trapper often just sets the snare in the animal's regular path, hoping that the snare will be invisible to the animal. The descriptions of snares and deadfalls below are rather brief or abstract, but it is important to have an overview of the concepts, although in actual practice it is the details that count.

In many cases, snares are more useful than deadfalls, partly for the above-mentioned reason that they usually do not require finding bait. For rabbits or hares, the snare would have either a flexible spring-pole or a nonflexible toss-pole; the latter sits in a fork that acts as a fulcrum. The noose itself is held in place either with a loop of the cord or by a tiny toggle-stick that serves the same triggering function. For larger animals the trap is much simpler, just a length of strong braided rawhide set in place in such a way that the animal sticks its head through the noose.

As long as metallic wire is still available, you might as well use it. Snares that use wire are less complicated than those that use natural materials, since no mechanism is needed for lifting the animal from the ground to prevent it from chewing the material. In northern regions it is snowshoe hares that are most commonly snared in this manner. They can only be snared in the winter, when they make distinct trails. You need copper or brass wire (or steel wire, which may be easier to find) between about 20 and 24 gauge. Some people use braided number-2 picture-hanging wire, but single-strand wire is fine. The snare wire should be about 50 cm long. Make a loop 10 cm wide, and fasten it to a well-fixed horizontal pole so that the bottom of the snare is 5 to 8 cm above the trail.

Although snares were generally used more often than deadfalls, in the desert areas of the southwestern US the opposite was the case, partly because of the available materials. The basic principal of making that type of deadfall is to place two large flat rocks so that they form a hinge, which is held open by a vertical stick or a set of sticks. The simplest form of rock deadfall, and in fact the one most commonly used for the smaller mammals, has the vertical stick held in place by nothing more than a kernel of dried corn underneath it.

Fishing

Another important source of animal food, of course, is fish (Rau, 1884; Rostlund, 1952; Stewart, 1977). They are an excellent source of protein, even though most of the freshwater varieties don't provide enough fat for a steady diet.

There are several good books on modern sport fishing available, and there would be little point in trying to include all that information here. For the most part, these methods involve a rod and a reel. From a survivalist perspective, perhaps all that should be added is that while the modern types of fishing gear include "spincast," "spinning," "baitcast," and "fly," the first is really more suitable for a beginner than for a more serious person, while the fourth is perhaps questionable as a survival tool since it is intended mainly for use with artificial bait. In general, natural baits are more effective than artificial ones, although it takes time to find such things.

I should also point out that along with the above types of gear, there is also the much simpler device of a pole of 3 to 4 m, with a line of the same length attached to one end, and with a hook, a float, and a weight at the other end of the line—with not much practice, such a rig might catch as many fish as more sophisticated gear.

There are many other ways to catch fish, and some of them are illegal nowadays in many areas, but in a true survival situation you might be forced to bend the rules. You might also end up using a torch or other fire to attract fish at night, and you wouldn't worry too much about sizes or catch limits. In fact, as a general rule of survival it often makes more sense to go after smaller prey: instead of using minnows to catch larger fish, why not eat the minnows yourself? They are eaten with pleasure in many countries, and they don't need gutting or beheading.

You can certainly use a hook and line to catch fish, as just mentioned, but this can sometimes be an inefficient way to get a meal. In any case, if one hook is good, then several hooks are better. A trotline is a strong cord tied from one side of a stream to another, or from one side of a stream or lake to one or more floats further out in the water. (The cord might simply be allowed to extend out and downwards into the water and held down at the far end with a weight—in which case the device might be regarded less as a horizontal "trotline" and more as a vertical "dropline.") From this strong cord are suspended shorter doubled cords called snoods, perhaps 30 cm long and 1 m apart, with a baited hook at the end of each snood. (You could also just tie a series of big loops in the main cord and use those as your snoods.) If available, a swivel should be used at either the top or bottom of each snood to prevent any fish from twisting the line, and a pair of clamps might be used on each snood to keep it separated from others. There might be a weight holding the centre of the main cord close to the bottom of the river. Trotlines are generally used for catfish, but anything from bass to turtles can be caught.

Other fishing methods include the use of traps,

spears, harpoons, bows and arrows, and nets. Sometimes fish can even be caught in slow-moving water by adding substances to the water that will poison or stun the fish without making it poisonous for humans: the Natives of North America used buckeye nuts, amole, turkey mullein, Indian hemp, pokeweed, Indian turnip, walnut bark, and devil's shoestring.

Primitive hooks can be made of wood, bone, antler, or shell. Some are made of one piece of material; some are made of two. One-piece bone hooks are made by first taking a large, flat piece of bone and scratching the curved design of the hook on it. By deepening these scratches, the hook can finally be lifted away from the rest of the bone. The hook is sanded to shape, and a groove is cut around the top of the shank to hold the line.

The two-piece kind of hook has several variations, but basically it involves tying a pointed bit of bone or hard wood—a thorn would also work—to a wooden shaft. The top of the shaft is carved to form a knob to hold the line, or a groove is cut around the shaft. Tie the string to the shaft, and weave it back and forth around the shaft and the point in a series of figure eights about a dozen times. If you make the hook entirely out of wood, you'll have to tie a small piece of stone or bone to the top of the shaft to get it to sink.

Another simple device used for catching fish is the gorge. Sharpen a sliver of bone at both ends, and carve a groove around the middle, or drill a hole through it, to hold the string. When the fish swallows the gorge, it turns sideways and catches.

The hook or gorge is fastened to a cord, which in turn is fastened to the end of a pole. Hooks and gorges can be baited with meat, fish, or insects. An artificial lure can be used instead; it is usually dangled from the end of a separate line.

Another kind of fish trap, very commonly used in aboriginal times, is the weir, basically a fence or wall built across a river. Often the weir is V-shaped, with the point of the V usually downstream, so that the force of the current carries the fish down into the centre. The point is kept open wide enough for the fish to swim through into some sort of corral. The Inuit made the trap (straight, not V-shaped) out of boulders placed across a shallow river, while further south the trap was usually made of poles planted in the riverbed.

An improvement on this setup is to place a basket trap at the point of the V. Basket traps can be made in all sizes, from about 1 m to over 6 m in length. To make one, take several dozen long, thin poles and fasten hoops either inside or outside them. Decrease the size of the hoops as you reach one end of the poles. Eventually, the ends of the poles should meet in order to close off one end of the trap. Tie the trap to the point of the V, with a few heavy rocks inside to hold it down on the bottom of the river.

Perhaps the most effective of all devices for fishing are nets, but they represent quite an advanced stage of "primitive" technology, especially if we consider that before the net can be made someone must produce great lengths of cordage. Again, only the basic idea can be presented here. Nets can take many forms, from dip nets to much larger seine nets that are drawn around whole schools of fish, but perhaps the most common is the gill net, so called because its mesh is large enough for a fish to put its head through, but small enough that it will get caught by the gills.

A gill net, or a rectangular fish net of any other sort, basically consists of several rows of sheet bends. (The first row, though, is a series of "half meshes," loops joined to a stronger main cord with either girth hitches or clove hitches.) You'll need a good deal of cord, perhaps 100 or 200 m, and a stronger cord to go all around the sides of the net. You'll also need a gauge for measuring the meshes, and a shuttle to hold the cord as you weave. The gauge is just a thin rectangular piece of wood about 10 cm long and perhaps 2 to 5 cm wide, depending on the average size of fish you expect to catch (northern fish are generally smaller); it is used to ensure that meshes are of uniform size. The shuttle is a flat piece of wood about 15 cm long and perhaps between 2 and 4 cm in width, with a deep notch at each end; the cord is wound onto the shuttle and then unwrapped as you go along (Blandford, 1961). The size of the mesh (usually defined as the distance between two knots on opposite sides of a stretched mesh) might be anywhere between 4 and 10 cm, depending on how large you expect the fish to be; the width of the gauge is half the size of the mesh.

Keep the meshes somewhat squeezed together, left to right, as you make them, so that the cord can be wrapped tightly around the gauge; you can spread the meshes out later. When you get to the end of the first row of sheet bends, go around to the other side of the net and start another row of meshes below the first—or learn to work in both directions. Continue in that manner until all the necessary rows have been completed, creating an overall pattern of diamonds (lozenges). All that is needed after that is to tie some floats along the top (perhaps made of wood or bark), and some weights (perhaps made from stones) along the bottom. But all of this is complicated and somewhat beyond basic "survival skills." Blandford's explanations (1961) are excellent.

However, a cruder but perhaps adequate gill net can be made even without a shuttle, and without even much knowledge of knots. All that is needed is two firm vertical posts to hold the work, a few metres of strong cord to hang the actual net on (with plenty of extra at each end so that the finished net can be tied in place when in use), and again a good deal of thinner cord. A gauge of some sort would be useful. Stretch the strong cord between the two posts. Cut the thinner cord into pieces about 2 m in length. Take each of these thinner pieces, fold it in half, drape the loop (bight) over the strong cord, and pull the two ends through that loop to make a girth hitch. Keep each of these looped pairs of cord at intervals of somewhere between 2 to 5 cm, again depending on the size of fish you expect to be dealing with. Then move your hands down by about that same of distance of 2 to 5 cm. Take the right-hand piece from one pair, and the left-hand piece from the next pair, hold the pieces parallel, and tie them together with a simple overhand knot. Continue that same process of tying pieces of cord together, moving from left to right along the entire distance of the main cord.

There are various ways of setting a gill net. If a creek is narrow enough, it might be possible to fasten the net right across from one bank to another. If not, then one end is tied to a tree or stake on the shore, and the far end is pulled out into the water by someone swimming or in a boat and fastened to a long pole planted in the river bed, or the end can be kept in place by a big float at the top and a big anchor-stone under the water, somewhat in the manner of setting a trotline. One good place to put a gill net is in a bend in a river, on the outside curve, preferably where the river widens slightly and has little whirlpools; fish often rest and feed in these spots.

Miscellaneous Wild-Animal Food

Almost any creature can provide food, but there are a few exceptions in North America. Some Pacific bivalves (e.g., mussels, oysters, and clams) are often dangerous in the summertime because of a poisonous organism that gets into them. You can eat most types of insects, but there are a few kinds to be avoided, mostly butterflies, moths, and adult beetles; the usual (and somewhat obvious) rule is that if it tastes bitter, it probably isn't digestible.

Insects are high in protein and certainly worth considering as food. The most practical insect dish is grasshoppers, which are a common item of food in many parts of the world. They are easiest to catch on a cold morning, when they are not moving very quickly. Catching grasshoppers can be a community affair; people can dig a pit near the grasshoppers, 1 or 2 m deep, and then make a big circle around the pit and the insects. They can then walk inwards towards the pit, hitting the ground with branches, forcing the grasshoppers to jump into the pit, from which they can be scooped up to be boiled or roasted. Roasted grasshoppers can later be crushed into a powder to be used in soup. Grasshoppers aren't bad tasting; they're a bit like unsalted peanuts.

Other sources of animal food are the many kinds of shellfish (Gibbons, 1964). Not only can the bivalves be eaten (except sometimes, as noted, on the Pacific coast during the summer), but also the univalves: periwinkles, whelks, and other kinds of snails. Mussels can just be picked up from the rocks, but clams require digging. An ordinary garden fork is a good tool for that. There are several kinds of clams, generally found below the surface of mud or sand, and each kind has its own preferred place to live. Some kinds prefer the high-tide zone, others prefer the low-tide zone. Some kinds live in mud; others prefer sand. The easiest way to spot clams is to watch for their squirts as you walk near them. When you see them spurting water in this way, dig a hole beside some of these spurts, and then start digging sideways towards the clams to get at them.

Reptiles and amphibians can be clubbed or speared for food. Snake is certainly a worthwhile emergency food; there isn't a great deal of meat on an average snake fillet, but it tastes fine. Turtles can be caught with just a piece of meat fastened to one end of a line, with the other end of the line tied to a pole stuck in the riverbank. Frogs are an excellent source of food. Bullfrogs can easily be speared from a canoe (split a stick partway, to make a two-pronged spear); most of the meat is on the back legs.

Grouse and other birds can be caught in snares, which might be set up in a circle around some grain thrown down as bait. Ducks and geese are most easily shot or corralled during the summer molting season, when they are less able to fly. A bola can be used to bring down birds from a passing flock. The bola is simply three rocks encased in leather pouches, which in turn are attached to cords joined together at the end. The cords are whirled around the head and let loose at the right moment.

Domesticated Animals

If you're determined to raise animals for food, you may find that chickens are the least troublesome, but do so in a simpler manner than that described by most of the modern books, which are based on maximized (commercialized) production. A chicken lays about one egg every day, so you wouldn't need many birds. You can feed them grains and greenery, but they'll eat practically anything. Even if you lose a few to predators, you should let your chickens run free, so that they can find a lot of their food by themselves. Chickens get calcium and phosphorus from the soil they eat; if your land is lacking these elements, you would have to use supplements such as mollusk shells or crushed limestone—but it might be impossible to obtain these. A coop, even if just a primitive one, must be built as a defence against predators. It would be best to find or create a breed of chicken that looked and acted like its early ancestors: strong but small even if not as productive as modern chickens in terms of meat or eggs.

If you're adventurous, you could try raising goats, sheep, or pigs, whereas cows might take up too much room. Without touching on all the complexities of animal husbandry, it might be worth pointing out that most of the modern textbooks on the subject are largely filled with descriptions of the various diseases of animals and the methods of treatment. If we look at the way domesticated animals are raised in pre-industrial societies, on the other hand, we can see that the most obvious difference is that treatment of disease is largely ignored. Any medieval European chronicle, for example, will say that in the year such-and-such the herds and flocks were wiped out by one nameless disease or another. These things used to be regarded as the unavoidable caprices of Nature, and even if human hunger was the consequence, the only solution was to wait for the disease to run its course.

Preserving Animal Food

Mammals should be bled and gutted soon after killing. The blood can be used to make soup, and the liver, kidneys, and most other organs should be eaten right away, since they can't be preserved easily. About the only organ that isn't edible is the gall bladder (although deer don't have one), next to the liver.

You can preserve fish by splitting them in half and hanging them up to dry in the sun, or a smoky fire can be built underneath. The flesh of larger fish can be slashed a few times to speed up the drying. Very small fish don't need to be split or gutted, but just strung up and smoked.

The flesh of mammals is treated in very much the same way as that of fish. In fairly warm and dry areas, the meat of deer or other mammals can be cut into strips and hung over poles to dry in the sun, but in other areas a small fire should be kept lit under the meat; the fire shouldn't heat the meat or even smoke it very much, just dry it out. The meat should be dried for several days, until it is somewhat leathery in texture, then packed away until it is needed, at which time it can be softened by boiling.

Preparing Hides

When you kill an animal, don't waste the hide. The following is how the Native people of North America prepared animal hides, although there were hundreds of variations on this method. The first task is to skin the animal (perhaps even before gutting): cut from the anus to the throat, along the inside of each leg, and around the head and feet. The sooner you do the skinning after killing the animal, the more easily the hide will come off, although the legs are always somewhat more difficult than other areas. Stretch the hide by pulling it repeatedly with your hands for an hour or so. If you want a more flexible product, mash and briefly simmer the animal's brain with a little water, and rub the mixture into the flesh side of the hide as you're stretching it. To prevent later attacks by vermin, suspend the hide above a smoky fire for an hour or so. The hides of rabbits and hares, however, need no treatment other than air-drying once they're removed from the animal.

The hides of deer and similar animals were usually treated somewhat differently: the hair tends to shed easily, so it is usually removed as the hide is being prepared. Begin by soaking the hide in lukewarm water for a few days until you can easily pull out handfuls of hair. Then throw the hide, with the hair side up, over the end of a big log that's been raised about 1 m above the ground at one end, and scrape off all the hair. Turn the hide over and scrape off all the remaining meat and fat. Continue with the usual process of stretching and twisting the hide to soften it, or use the animal's brain as described above. Since a deer hide is large and clumsy, another way to stretch it is to roll it up, tie it all in a big overhand knot, and then insert two short poles that can be twisted in opposite directions, tied together, and left for several hours. The last stage of preparation again might be to smoke the hide to protect it from vermin.

30
The Cycle of Civilization

From a Darwinian perspective, civilizations are rather brief interludes in the story of humankind. *Homo sapiens* and other members of our genus have walked the Earth at various times over the course of about 2 million years, but civilizations have existed for only about 5,000 years. Humanity's "uncivilized" past, therefore, is greater than its "civilized" phase by the enormous ratio of 400:1. Considering the brevity of the latter, it might almost be said that civilization is merely an experiment, the results of which are not entirely clear.

All civilizations grow too large to support themselves, and their leaders have little foresight. These civilizations then collapse and are buried in the mud. The fall of the Roman Empire, for example, has been ascribed to various factors, from laziness to lead poisoning. The impoverishment of the soil, and the consequent lack of food, may have played a large part. No doubt it was also a combined military and economic problem: there wasn't enough money to pay for all the soldiers guarding the frontiers. Pestilence may have been another significant factor. Perhaps a more correct answer would actually be a more general one: the empire was too big, and it was poorly led.

The main difference between the past and the future is that the cycle of "civilization" can no longer be repeated. Oil is not the only mineral that will be in short supply in the twenty-first century. Industrial civilization has always been dependent on metals, but hematite, for example, is no longer sufficiently common, and mining companies now look for other sources of iron, which can be processed only with modern machinery. In fact, most metals are globally now either declining or heading in that direction.

The technology of one century built the technology of the next. The technology of the past—the hammer, anvil, forge, and bellows of the ancient blacksmith— made it possible for later generations to extract the low-grade ores of the present. Very low-grade iron ores, for example, can now be worked, but only because there were once better, more accessible ores. This "mechanical evolution" is, of course, liable to collapse: when Rome fell, so did literacy, education, and technology. Eventually that knowledge was recovered, though, because the natural world was fundamentally unchanged.

In the future, however, after the collapse of the present civilization, the necessary fuels and ores will not be available for that gradual rebuilding of advanced technology. The loss of both petroleum and accessible ores means that history will no longer be a cycle of civilizations.

By the year 2100 there will not be many humans left, and those who hope to stay alive will have to approach the matter of their survival as if planning the colonization of a distant planet. But the collapse of industrial society may have a happy ending of some sort, or at least a semblance of redemption. The somewhat upbeat ending to the story is that there will be, so to speak, a "return to Nature."

In many ways the most important event in the development of humankind was not the transition from the Stone Age to civilization, but rather from the Paleolithic (the Old Stone Age) to the Neolithic (the New Stone Age). Specifically, the major event was the shift from foraging (hunting and gathering) to agriculture. Ultimately this event was a bad choice. Even at the present time, among surviving primitive societies, one can see that foraging has advantages over agriculture.

As Richard Lee (1968) and Brian Ferguson (2003, July/August) have both explained, there are many disadvantages to agricultural life. In the first place, agriculture does not generally lead to leisure and the consequent opportunity for intellectual refinement, contrary to popular belief. If there is any leisure, it is only for those at the top, whose easy life is dependent on the less-easy life of those at the bottom. Foragers, on the other hand, spend only about 20 hours a week on actual work.

Secondly, with agriculture and permanent settlements come the woes of social inequity: foragers are nomadic because of the cycle of the seasons, so they have little means of storing and transporting food, and in any case little need to do so, whereas the settled life of agriculture allows the rulers to accumulate food and hence other forms of wealth produced by the workers.

Thirdly, agricultural societies generally include violence in all its forms, because the wealth of the elite provides a motive for robbery within the state, and for warfare between one state and another.

Fourthly, agriculture is destructive to the environment: it causes soil depletion and desertification.

Finally, agriculture leads to poor health, at least in the sense that people who live mainly on grains are less healthy than those who live on a highly varied diet of wild plants and the flesh of wild animals.

The theory that the Paleolithic was better than the Neolithic is far from proven, of course. If we look at various societies, past and present, it may not be the case that they can all be divided into "happy foragers" and "unhappy farmers." Nor does it seem absolutely clear that foragers always work less than farmers: part of the problem there is that in any society the dividing line between (food-related) work and non-work is not always easily defined, so measurements are uncertain. Some of these controversies might be a matter of overgeneralization: it may well be, for example, that foraging requires less work but that some foraging societies are nevertheless violent.

Also in favour of the theory of the "happy forager," however, is the matter of our present ideological fallacies. Nowadays it is largely assumed, without any real evidence, that human life gets better from one century to the next. The belief in "progress," however, has not always been a common assumption. In fact, it really dates only from the eighteenth century, the so-called Age of Enlightenment, the birth of industrialism. Nevertheless the belief in progress now has a great hold on many people, and to a large extent it acts as a substitute for religion. The basic tenet is that humanity has gone from an unhappy world of savagery to a happy world of industrialism.

Yet as soon as we start to question this belief, its illogicality is obvious. Even in "developed" countries, there are the billionaires and the homeless. Warfare and general political strife are rampant, and there seems to be no such thing as honest government anywhere. The modern business world makes a mockery of our beliefs in democracy and equality: to succeed in business one must often be ruthless, unscrupulous, and devoid of a conscience. And instead of living a life of leisure, the average moderner tries desperately to find enough minutes to maintain a home, a family, and a job. Where, then, are the rewards of civilization? In an afterlife?

We must consider further implications of a belief in the Paleolithic ideal. In the first place, it is one thing to say that the Paleolithic was a happier time; it is another to say that people now living in technologically advanced societies should revert to Paleolithic ways of living. To do so, it would be necessary for the human population of Earth to drop from its present level of 7 billion to about 10 million, as it was toward the end of the Paleolithic, i.e., to shrink to much less than 1 percent of its present size. In addition, the Earth no longer has the abundance in flora and fauna that it had 10,000 years ago, so foraging would no longer be as easy as before. Finally, even if foraging is easier than farming, the average person living in industrial society nowadays has not been raised to a physically active life and by adulthood is probably permanently incapable of anything but a sedentary occupation.

A reply to this question of the logical consequences might be that if civilization in general will come to an end, the difficulties must simply be dealt with, although it will certainly take more than one generation to make the transition. A theory of a post-industrial primitive culture might require a great stretch of the imagination, but human cultures have always been capable of variation.

A further thought is that a return to the Paleolithic is, in any case, inevitable. Individual civilizations have come and gone over the last 5,000 years, but eventually civilization as we know it will come to a permanent end. Civilization destroys its own environment: already there are far too many humans, natural resources such as metals and fossil fuels are starting to decline, and arable land is crowded and less fertile. From the first civilization to the present day is a rather short time, compared to the 2 million years of hominid evolution. In the not-so-distant future, all that we now call civilization will be regarded merely as an aberration in the foraging way of life to which *Homo sapiens* is better suited.

When we lose our fossil fuels, we will have to go back at least as far as to an agrarian way of life. But that's just the first half of the problem. The other is that agriculture itself is just not "sustainable," if I may use a frequently misleading word ("sustainable" for a week? for a million years?). That is to say, agriculture causes the destruction of arable land: the more we farm, the more the farmland becomes eroded. "Organic" farming and similar practices can reduce the rate of loss, but only to a certain extent: elements such as phosphorus and calcium get washed away, no matter how we try to rationalize our behaviour. The result is ever-increasing famine.

The only way of life, therefore, that is in any way "sustainable" (although again there is that vague word) is foraging: hunting and gathering. But there is even more to the story, a psychological consideration, namely that walking around naked like the Australian aborigines may be simply too depressing to think about. We have been led to believe that the (foraging) life of humans in a state of Nature is "solitary, poor, nasty, brutish, and short," as Hobbes said three centuries ago. It turned out not to be true, but nothing will stop the popular belief in the greater blessings of farming (not foraging) life.

Even then, that foraging way of life will not last for eternity, because the cave dwellers of the future are eventually going to increase their numbers. So then the whole game will start over again. But it's also true that it took hominids the long space of 2 million years to get from zero to a population of 10 million, after which it was agriculture that fostered a much greater leap in the birth rate. So perhaps, after the end of civilization, *Homo sapiens* can once again maintain a small population for millions of years.

Over the course of the next few decades, all that is certain is that the future of humanity will start to resemble its distant past, except that much of the natural resources will be missing. However, the planet will still have about 100 million square kilometres of wilderness, ravaged though parts of it may be, and the "economy" in the depths of that natural world will be the same one that has been there for millions of years.

The intelligent thing to do would be to take control of that transition, to enter the future with both eyes open. Finding a new world for tomorrow means finding a way of life that is more attuned to the land, the sea, and the sky. There is no way for a small group of people to prevent systemic collapse, but it may be that things will be better when the collapse is completed. At the moment, there is only one direction, and that is out. We must literally step out of the present economy—and by "we" I mean those few who are clever enough to be saved, those few who make the effort to pack their bags. We must stop being part of "society." The details are uncertain, but the general picture is not too hard to draw. I envision a world where people can wake up each morning and greet the sunrise. I imagine a world in which people can live with nobility, dignity, and grace.

Appendix One
Energy

Modern industrial society is composed of a triad of fossil fuels, metals, and electricity. The three are intricately connected. Electricity, for example, can be generated on a global scale only with fossil fuels. The same dependence on fossil fuels is true of metals; in fact, the better types of ore are now becoming depleted, while those that remain can be processed only with modern machinery and require more fossil fuels for smelting. In turn, without metals and electricity, there will be no means of extracting and processing fossil fuels. Of the three members of the triad, electricity is the most fragile, and its failure will serve as an early warning of trouble with the other two (Duncan, 2000, November 13; 2005–06, Winter).

Often the interactions of this triad are hiding in plain sight. Global production of steel, for example, requires 420 million tonnes of coke (from coal) annually, as well as other fossil fuels adding up to an equivalent of another 100 million tonnes (Smil, 2009, September 17). To maintain industrial society, the production of steel cannot be curtailed: there are no "green" materials for the construction of skyscrapers, large bridges, automobiles, machinery, or tools.

But the interconnections among fossil fuels, metals, and electricity are innumerable. As each of the three members of the triad threatens to break down, we are looking at a society that is far more primitive than the one to which we have been accustomed.

Oil

One reasonable description of past and future global oil production is Campbell and Laherrère's 1998 *Scientific American* article "The End of Cheap Oil," which serves as a sort of *locus classicus*. Their main chart seems to indicate an annual rate of increase of about 4 percent from the year 1930 to 2000, and an annual rate of post-peak decline of slightly over 3 percent, which would mean that around 2030 oil production will be down to about half of the peak amount (Campbell & Laherrère, 1998, March). The chart is based partly on the bell-shaped curves that M. King Hubbert used in the 1950s when making accurate predictions of American and global oil decline (Grove, 1974, June; Hubbert, 1956).

Most major studies place the date of "peak oil" somewhere between 2000 and 2020 (Campbell, 2004, 2009, November 16; Gever et al., 1991; Oil Drum, 2010, February 4; Oxford University, 2010, March 23; Petrole, 2010, March 25; Simmons, 2006; Youngquist, 2000, October; 2008). For years the main anomalies have been some American government forecasts: those of the Energy Information Administration (EIA) of the US Department of Energy, and those of the US Geological Survey. However, Robert L. Hirsch of the US Department of

Energy in 2005 produced "The Inevitable Peaking of World Oil Production," the famous "Hirsch Report," which begins with the sentence, "The era of plentiful, low-cost petroleum is reaching an end." He goes on to say that "oil production is in decline in 33 of the world's 48 largest oil-producing countries" (Hirsch, 2005, October, p. 5). The EIA's 2009 "Sweetnam Report," in fact, shows world oil beginning a permanent decline in 2012, although the wording is somewhat ambiguous (EIA, 2009, April 7). Colin Campbell (2009, November 16) has responded to this report. Another anomaly has been that of the International Energy Agency, which has tended to follow US figures, but they later revised their claims (Macalister, 2009, November 9).

Of course, even within all those ranges, there are all sorts of other variations. Is it possible that fuels outside the range of conventional oil can make a significant difference? To what extent will enhanced production methods (water flooding, etc.) result in a "cliff" rather than a "slope"? How would a major financial recession (i.e., one not caused by oil scarcity), resulting in lowered demand, affect both production and prices? The biggest problem may be the synergism of fossil fuels, electricity, and metals: as one of the three declines, there is a decline of the other two, and the result is a chain reaction, a feedback mechanism, a tailspin, or whatever metaphor one chooses, so that industry in general comes to a sudden halt. Perhaps some of these unknowns will work out to be either irrelevant or identical in the long run, at least in the sense that (e.g.) a cliff and a slope both end at rock bottom.

Unconventional oil will not make a great difference to the final production numbers. By far the largest deposits of usable unconventional oil are the Canadian tar sands. The popular belief that "there's enough oil there to last a hundred years" is a good example of a modern half-truth. There are probably about 175 billion barrels of reserves (usable oil after processing), but there are two serious problems. The first is the rate of production: by the year 2020 it may be possible to increase production to 1.5 billion barrels a year; at such a slow rate of production, the reserves would indeed last a hundred years, but such figures are dwarfed by those for conventional oil and by the annual demands for oil. The second problem is that processing the tar sands requires enormous quantities of water and natural gas: the environmental damage is unparalleled, and it might be impossible to supply such quantities anyway (Foucher, 2009, February 25; Hall, 2008, April 15).

From a broader perspective it can be said that, as oil declines, more energy and money must be devoted to getting the less-accessible and lower-quality oil out of the ground (Gever et al., 1991). In turn, as more energy and money are devoted to oil production, the production of metals and electricity becomes more difficult. One problem feeds on another.

It should also be remembered that the quest for the date of peak oil is in some respects a red herring. In terms of daily life, it is important to consider not only peak oil in the absolute sense, but peak oil per capita. The date of the latter was 1979, when there were 5.5 barrels of oil per person annually, as opposed to 4.3 in 2009 (BP, annual).

The problem of the world's diminishing supply of oil is a problem of energy, not a problem of money. The old bromide that "higher prices will eventually make [e.g.] shale oil economically feasible" is meaningless. This planet has only a finite amount of fossil fuel. That fuel is starting to vanish, and "higher prices" will be quite unable to stop the event from taking place (Hanson, 1999, Spring).

Coal

The assessment of coal production is complicated by the fact that there is a huge difference between "peak coal mass" and "peak coal energy." In other words, the coal that is being mined today is much lower in quality than the coal of earlier years. In addition, there are great uncertainties as to how much coal is really still in the ground.

The future of coal will resemble that of oil. The energy content of US coal has been going down since at least 1950, because the hard coal (anthracite and bituminous coal) is becoming depleted and must be replaced by sub-bituminous coal and lignite. Anthracite production in the US has been in decline since 1990. For those reasons, the actual energy output of all US coal has been flat since that same date. New technologies and mining methods cannot compete against the problems of lower-quality ore and more-difficult seams.

Actual production in the US might reach a plateau of 1,400 Mt annually and stay there for the rest of the century. That will happen, however, only if there is massive development of the reserves in Montana, and if serious problems of transportation and the environment can be dealt with. Otherwise, US production will peak around 2030 (Höök & Aleklett, 2009, May 1).

The US has almost 30 percent of the world's coal reserves, while China has only the third-largest reserves, totalling 14 percent, but China accounts for 43 percent of the world's production (Höök et al., 2010, June 8). With its enormous growth in consumption, it is unlikely that China's coal supply will last until 2030 (Heinberg, 2009; 2010, May).

Worldwide, coal production is estimated to peak around 2020, to judge from historical production and proved reserves. Estimations based on a logistic (Hubbert) curve give almost the same result. Even if we assume, with great optimism, that ultimate reserves will be double the present proved reserves, such amounts would only delay the peak by a few years; even then, if production rates increase accordingly, the duration of the reserves will remain about the same (Höök et al., 2010, June 8). In terms of energy (vs. mass), the Energy Watch Group (2007, July 10) predicts the peak of global coal production to be around 2025.

Hydroelectricity

The first problem with hydroelectricity is that all the big rivers have been dammed already; also, the dams silt up and become useless after a few years (Youngquist, 2000, October). Decentralization, i.e., putting dams on smaller rivers, would solve nothing; on the contrary, decentralization leads to inefficiency—that is why the small hydro generators were closed down in the first place. The damage that the dams cause to wildlife and farmland is considerable. In addition, the end product is only electricity, which is not a practical substitute for the fossil fuels now used in transportation. The final problem is that as fossil fuels and metals disappear, there will be no means of making the parts to repair old generators or to build new ones.

Nuclear Power

Nuclear power presents significant environmental dangers, but the biggest constraints involve the addition of new reactor capacity and the supply of uranium. Peak production of uranium ore in the US was in 1980. Mainly because the US was the world's largest producer, the peak of global production was at approximately the same date (Energy Watch Group, 2006, December; Storm van Leeuwen, 2008, February). Statements that uranium ore is abundant are based on the falsehood that all forms of uranium ore are usable. In reality, only high-quality ore serves any purpose, whereas low-quality ore presents the unsolvable problem of negative net energy: the mining and milling of such ore requires more energy than is derived from the actual use of the ore in a reactor. The world's usable uranium ore will probably be finished by about 2030, and there is no evidence for the existence of large new deposits of rich ore. Claims of abundant uranium are generally made by industry spokespersons whose positions are far from neutral, who have in fact a vested interest in presenting nuclear energy as a viable option (Storm van Leeuwen, 2008, February). One must also beware, of course, of the myth that "higher prices" will make low-grade resources of any sort feasible: when net energy is negative, even an infinitely higher price will not change the balance. For all practical purposes, the nuclear industry will come to an end in a matter of decades, not centuries.

Energy and Electricity

Global production of all forms of energy for the year 2005 was about 500 exajoules (EJ), most of which was supplied by fossil fuels. This annual production of energy can also be expressed in terms of billion barrels of oil equivalent (bboe) (BP, annual; Duncan, 2000, November 13; 2005–06, Winter; EIA, 2008, December 31). In 1990 this was 59.3 bboe, and in 2005 it was 79.3, an increase of 34 percent.

However, the use of electricity worldwide rose from 11,865.4 terawatt-hours in 1990 to 18,301.8 in 2005 (BP, annual), an increase of 54 percent. Since the use of electricity is rising much more quickly than the total production of energy, it is uncertain whether in the future there will be sufficient energy to meet the demand for electricity. If not, there could be widespread brownouts and rolling blackouts (Duncan, 2000, November 13; 2005–06, Winter). When electricity starts to go, so will everything else.

Alternative Energy

Solutions based on theories of alternative energy ignore, among other things, the infrastructure upon which a theoretical world of "alternative" energy would be based. To understand the problem of infrastructure entirely, we need to look at it as a loop, a matter of bootstrapping—the metaphors are numerous. To what extent, indeed, is it possible to raise oneself off the ground by pulling on one's own bootlaces? The various answers to such a question can provide support either for or against the use of alternative sources of energy. The question of the "bootstrapping" of alternative energy may be either ontologically profound or utterly naïve, depending on how it is phrased, but actually it is rarely asked. At the risk of playing the devil's advocate, however, I might point out two cases.

The first is somewhat general: many of the devices using advanced technology for alternative energy (e.g., solar-powered devices, wind turbines) operate at their present levels of efficiency only because of the use of alloys that include rare-earth metals. Without fossil fuels, it would therefore be necessary to use (e.g.) solar-powered devices—or devices ultimately powered by other devices similarly powered—to roam the earth in search of these materials. Other solar-powered devices would then do the mining and milling. Further devices of a similar nature would be used to manufacture solar-powered equipment from these metals, and these last devices would then continue that technological cycle. All of this, of course, would have to be in place worldwide in the few years before fossil fuels have largely vanished. Although from what might be called a philosophical perspective there is nothing wrong with such a scenario, it seems obvious that one is leaving reality far behind.

A second, less bizarre example might be the following: would it not be possible to solve the original problem of the manufacture, transportation, maintenance, and repair of equipment by establishing a worldwide grid annually carrying 500 EJ of electricity that could be delivered wherever it was needed? If so, then one might well imagine large trucks rolling along the highways, their wheels powered by large batteries. The answer, unfortunately, is that a battery for any large vehicle would have unsolvable problems of weight, longevity, temperature, and so on. There is also the much bigger question of where the 500 EJ would be coming from in the first place.

Appendix Two
Resources

Minerals

Global depletion of minerals other than petroleum and uranium is somewhat difficult to determine, partly because recycling complicates the issues, partly because trade goes on in all directions, and partly because one material can sometimes be replaced by another. All that is fairly certain is that there is not enough usable copper, zinc, and platinum on the planet Earth, even with improved recycling and better technology, for the world's "developing countries" to use as much per capita as the US (Gordon et al., 2006, January 31).

Figures from the US Geological Survey indicate that within the US most types of minerals are past their peak dates of production. Besides oil, these include bauxite (peaking in 1943), copper (1998), iron ore (1951), magnesium (1966), phosphate rock (1980), potash (1967), rare earth metals (1984), tin (1945), titanium (1964), and zinc (1969) (USGS, 2005). The depletion of all minerals in the US continues swiftly in spite of recycling.

L. David Roper (2012, January 12) estimates that globally the peak of the reserve base (i.e., including reserves not currently economic) for bauxite (for aluminum) production will be around 2040, for copper around 2030, and for iron ore around 2020.

Iron ore may seem infinitely abundant, but it is not. In the past it was ores such as natural hematite (Fe_2O_3) that were being mined. For thousands of years, also, tools were produced by smelting bog iron, mainly goethite, $FeO(OH)$, in clay cylinders only 1 m or so in height. Modern mining must rely more heavily on taconite, a flintlike ore containing less than 30 percent magnetite and hematite (Gever et al., 1991). Iron ore of the sort that can be processed with primitive equipment is becoming scarce, in other words, and only the less-tractable forms such as taconite will be widely available when the oil-powered machinery has disappeared. With the types of iron ore used in the past, it will be easy enough to reproduce at least the medieval level of black-smithing in future ages. With taconite it will not.

Grain

Annual world production of grain per capita peaked in 1984 at 342 kg (Brown, 2006, June 15). For years production has not met demand, so carry-over stocks must fill the gap, now leaving less than two months' supply as a buffer. Rising temperatures and falling water tables are causing havoc in grain harvests everywhere, but the biggest dent is caused by the biofuel industry, which is growing at over 20 percent per year. In 2007, 88 million tons of US corn, a quarter of the entire US harvest, were turned into automotive fuel.

Fish

The world catch of wild fish per capita peaked in 1988 at 17 kg; by 2005 it was down to 14 kg (Larsen, 2005, June 22). The fishing industry sends out 4 million vessels to catch wild fish, but stocks of the larger species are falling rapidly, so the industry works its way steadily down the food chain. Larsen notes in particular that "over the past 50 years, the number of large predatory fish in the oceans has dropped by a startling 90 percent. Catches of many popular food fish such as cod, tuna, flounder, and hake have been cut in half despite a tripling in fishing effort" (2005, June 22, p. 1).

The losses in the production of wild fish are made up by aquaculture (fish farming), but aquaculture causes its own problems: inshore fish farms entail the destruction of wetlands, spread diseases, and deplete oxygen. Although her study is otherwise excellent, Larsen omits the fact that millions of tonnes of other fish must be turned into food every year for use in aquaculture. The Food and Agriculture Organization (FAO) dismisses these as "low-value/trash fish" (2006).

Arable Land

Land may be unsuitable for agriculture for many reasons (Bot et al., 2000). The climate may be too dry, too wet (not well drained), too hot, or too cold. There may be too much rain or too much snow. The terrain may be too mountainous. The soil may be nutrient-poor or polluted.

Soils may be naturally infertile for several reasons. They may have a low organic content; generally these are very sandy soils. There may be toxic levels of naturally occurring aluminum, resulting in acidity. There may be a deficiency in available phosphorus if it is bound to ferric oxides (Fe_2O_3). Soils may be vertic (consisting of cracking clays), saline (containing NaCl), sodic (containing Na_2CO_3), or just too shallow.

The rest constitutes the world's "potential arable land." To judge from the FAO Soil Map of the World, it would appear that the potential arable land is 38,488,090 km^2, less than a third of the world's total land area. This figure refers both to the land now being utilized for agriculture and to the remaining land (net potential arable) that might be used in the future. The utilized arable land constitutes about 15,000,000 km^2. (Bot et al., [2000] estimate 14,633,840 km^2. The CIA [2010] estimates 10.57 percent of a total land surface of 149,000,000 km^2, therefore presumably about 15,749,300 km^2.) It would appear, then, that only about 38 percent of the world's potential arable land is actually being used, and that there is a "land balance" (the cultivable but non-cultivated land) of 62 percent. (All of this is based on the assumption that any increase in cultivated land will happen without irrigation, since water is already in short supply.)

Bot et al., however, point out that for several reasons the figures from this map may be unrealistic. In the first place, a great deal of the land now being used is degraded, although the extent and degree of degradation of arable land are not entirely certain. The UNEP Global Assessment of Human-Induced Soil Degradation does not distinguish arable from non-arable land, but 41 countries have over 60 percent of their land (both arable and non-arable) severely degraded. Degradation is caused by deforestation, by overgrazing, by overexploitation of vegetation (e.g., for firewood or timber), and by industrial activities (pollution). Agricultural activities themselves lead to soil degradation. Secondly, the unused arable land in developing countries is more than half forest. Cutting down forest would cause its own problems: the forest is in itself a valuable resource, and cutting it down would lead to wind and water erosion. Thirdly, much arable land is already being used for grazing. A more realistic estimate may be that the "land balance" is only somewhere between 3 and 25 percent.

What, then, constitutes the extent of "potential arable land"? On the positive side, there are parts of the world where the area of cultivated land might be increased. To do so, however, it would be necessary to destroy forests or other wilderness. Also on the negative side is the problem of soil degradation in the land that is now being cultivated. But that is not a straightforward matter: some land is very degraded, some is not so degraded, and the amount of land in each degree of severity varies from one country to another. At what point is land so degraded that it should no longer be labelled "arable land"? And the next question is: what is the net result of the positive and the negative? It would seem that the two roughly balance each other out.

Fresh Water

Fresh water is declining in many countries around the world, particularly Mexico, the western US, North Africa, the Middle East, Pakistan, India, China, and Australia. If there is no population crash in the next few years, by the year 2025 about 2 billion people will be living with extreme water scarcity, and about two-thirds of the world will be facing water shortages to some extent (UN Environment Program, 2007). In Saudi Arabia and the adjacent countries from Syria to Oman, the annual water supply per capita fell from 1,700 m^3 to 907 m^3 between 1985 and 2005. In the countries of the Gulf Cooperation Council, most fresh water is supplied by desalination plants (UN Environment Program, 2007).

The diversion of water for agriculture and municipal use is causing rivers to run dry. The Colorado, the Ganges, the Nile, and the Indus are now all dry for at least part of the year before they reach the sea. In previous years, this was also true of China's Yellow River; whether better management will prevail remains to be seen. The Amu Darya, once the largest river flowing into the Aral Sea, now runs dry as its water is diverted for the cultivation of cotton (Mygatt, 2006, July 26).

Most countries with water shortages are pumping at rates that cannot be maintained. The shallower aquifers could be replenished if pumping were reduced, but the deeper "fossil" aquifers cannot be rejuvenated when their levels are allowed to fall. Among the latter are the US Ogallala aquifer, the Saudi aquifer, and the deeper aquifer of the North China Plain (Brown, 2008).

Agriculture uses more than 70 percent of the world's fresh water and is mainly responsible for the depletion of aquifers of both types (UN Environment Program, 2007). World grain harvests tripled between 1950 and 2000, but only with increases in irrigation. The US depends on irrigation for a fifth of its grain production; in parts of the grain-producing states of Texas, Oklahoma, and Kansas the water table has fallen more than 30 m, and thousands of wells have gone dry (Brown, 2008). The situation is worse in China, where four-fifths of the grain harvest depends on irrigation. The fossil aquifer of the North China Plain maintains half of China's wheat production and a third of its corn. As a result of the depletion of water, Chinese annual grain production has been in decline since 1998.

All this excess use of water is leading to political strife. While the seas have long been generally subject to international laws, it is only in recent decades that there have been major international problems with the world's fresh water. Because of falling water levels, new wells are drilled to greater depths than the old, with the result that the owners of the old wells are left without water. The result is a cycle of competition in which no one wins.

A similar competition exists with the world's rivers. Sixty percent of the world's 227 largest rivers have numerous dams and canals, and there are not many other rivers that are entirely free from such obstructions (UN Environment Program, 2007). Most countries sharing a large river with others are in the midst of violent struggle or about to become so. For example, India's Farakka Barrage, completed in 1975, diverts water from the Ganges into its Indian tributary, thereby depriving Bangladesh of water (Smith & Vivekananda, 2007, November). Egypt and Sudan signed a treaty in 1959 allocating 75 percent of the Nile's water to the former and the remainder to Sudan, with no provisions for the other countries through which the river flows, and Egypt has threatened military action against any of those countries if their irrigation projects reduce the flow (Elhadj, 2008, September).

It is not only military strength that settles issues of water distribution: countries with more water can produce more grain and thus influence the economies of less fortunate countries. It takes a thousand tonnes of water to produce a tonne of grain. In the short term it may therefore seem more sensible for water-poor countries to stop depleting their water by producing grain and instead buy it from water-rich countries (Brown, 2008; UN Environment Program, 2007). Between 1984 and 2000, at a cost of about $100 billion, Saudi Arabia foolishly tried to produce its own grain but then gave up and switched to importing it. Buying grain has its own negative side effects, however, in terms of national security, foreign exchange, and lost local employment (Elhadj, 2008, September). The biggest question of national security, however, may be: what will happen when the grain-exporting countries themselves start running out of both grain and water?

References

Aguirre, F. (2005, October 29). Thoughts on urban survival (post-collapse life in Argentina). *Free Republic*. Retrieved from http://freerepublic.com/focus/news/1511641/posts?page=116

Aleklett, K. (2007, June 5). Severe climate change unlikely before we run out of fossil fuel. Online Opinion. Retrieved from www.onlineopinion.com.au

Anonymous. (2007, February 13). *Thoughts on disaster survival*. Retrieved from www.frfrogspad.com/disastr.htm

Bagdikian, B. H. (2004). *The new media monopoly*. 6th ed. Boston: Beacon Press.

Bailey, L. H. (1910). *Manual of gardening*. New York: Macmillan.

Bede. (1962). *Historical Works*. Trans. J. E. King. 2 vols. Cambridge, Massachusetts: Harvard University Press.

Beers, M. H., Editor-in-Chief. (2003). *The Merck manual of medical information*. 2nd home ed. New York: Pocket Books.

Blandford, P. W. (1961). *Netmaking*. Glasgow: Brown, Son & Ferguson.

Booker, C. (2008, June 10). Fuel crisis: Forget warnings of panic at the pumps. Britain is set to lose nearly half its electricity in six years. *Daily Mail*. Retrieved from www.dailymail.co.uk/news/article-1025586/FUEL-CRISIS-Forget-warnings-panic-pumps-Thanks-decades-government- neglect-Britain-set-lose-nearly-half-electricity-years.html

Bot, A. J., Nachtergaele, F. O., & Young, A. (2000). *Land resource potential and constraints at regional and country levels*. World Soil Resources Reports 90. Rome: Land and Water Development Division, FAO. Retrieved from www.fao.org/ag/agl/agll/terrastat/

BP. (Annual). *Global statistical review of world energy*. Retrieved from www.bp.com/statisticalreview

Bradley, F. M., & Ellis, B. W., eds. (1992). *Rodale's all-new encyclopedia of organic gardening*. Emmaus, Pennyslvania: Rodale.

Broadfoot, B. (1997). *Ten lost years 1929–1939: Memories of Canadians who survived the Depression*. Toronto: McClelland & Stewart.

Brown, L. (2006, June 15). Grain harvest. Earth Policy Indicators. Retrieved from www.earthpolicy.org/index.php?/indicators/C54/

Brown, L. (2008). *Plan B: Mobilizing to save civilization*. New York: Norton & Co.

Buchman, D. D. (1996). *Herbal medicine*. Rev. ed. New York: Gramercy Publishing.

Campbell, C. J. (2004). *The coming oil crisis*. Brentwood, Essex: Multi-Science Publishing Company.

Campbell, C. J. (2009, November 16). Colin Campbell's response to the Guardian IEA reporting. *The Oil Drum*. Retrieved from www.theoildrum.com/node/5970

Campbell, C. J., & Laherrère, J. H. (1998, March). The end of cheap oil. *Scientific American*.

Carter, G. (2009, January 15). Credibility crunch hits Iron Age building. Retrieved from http://structuralarchaeology. blogspot.ca/2009/01/18-credibility-crunch-hits-iron-age.html

Carter, V. G., & Dale, T. (1974). *Topsoil and civilization*. Rev. ed. Norman, Oklahoma: University of Oklahoma Press.

Catton, W. R., Jr. (1982). *Overshoot: The ecological basis of revolutionary change*. Champaign, Illinois: University of Illinois Press.

CIA. (2010). *World factbook*. US Government Printing Office. Retrieved from https://www.cia.gov/library/publications/the-world-factbook

Cooper, J. M. (1978). *Snares, deadfalls, and other traps of the northern Algonquians and northern Athapaskans*. Reprint. New York: AMS Press.

Deputy W. (2009, January). *The thin blue line*. Survival Blog. Retrieved from www.survivalblog.com/2009/01/ the_thin_ blue_line_by_deputy_w.html

Dunbar, R. I. M. (1992). Neocortex size as a constraint on group size in primates. *Journal of Human Evolution, 20* (6), 469–93. Retrieved from www.sciencedirect.com/science/article/pii/ 004724849290081J

Duncan, R. C. (2000, November 13). The peak of world oil production and the road to the Olduvai Gorge. Geological Society of America, Summit 2000. Reno, Nevada. Retrieved from www.dieoff.org/page224.htm

Duncan, R. C. (2005–06, Winter). The Olduvai theory: Energy, population, and industrial civilization. *The Social Contract*. Retrieved from www.thesocialcontract.com/pdf/sixteen- two/xvi-2-93.pdf

EIA. (2008, December 31). World consumption of primary energy by energy type and selected country groups. Retrieved from www.eia.doe.gov/pub/international/ieaLf/table18.xls

EIA. (2009, April 7). *Meeting the world's demand for liquid fuels: A roundtable discussion, a new climate for energy*. EIA 2009 Energy Conference. Retrieved from www.eia.doe.gov/ conference/2009/session3/Sweetnam.pdf

Elhadj, E. (2008, September). Dry aquifers in Arab countries and the looming food crisis. *The Middle East Review of International Affairs, 12* (3). Retrieved from https:// whitelocust.wordpress.com/dry-aquifers-in-arab-countries- and-the-looming-food-crisis/

Energy Watch Group. (2006, December). *Uranium resources and nuclear energy*. EWG-Series No. 1. Retrieved from www.lbst. de/ressources/docs2006/EWG-paper_1-06_Uranium- Resources-Nuclear-Energy_03DEC2006.pdf

Energy Watch Group. (2007, July 10). Coal: Resources and future production. EWG-Series No 1. Retrieved from www.energy-watchgroup.org/fileadmin/global/pdf/EWG_Report_Coal_10-07-2007ms.pdf

FAO. (2006). *The state of world fisheries and aquaculture 2006*. Retrieved from www.fao.org/docrep/009/A0699e/A0699E00.htm

Ferguson, R. B. (2003, July/August). The birth of war. *Natural History*. Retrieved from http://iweb.tntech.edu/kosburn/history-444/birth_of_war.htm

Foucher, S. (2009, February 25). Analysis of decline rates. *The Oil Drum*. Retrieved from http://iseof.org/pdf/theoildrum_4820.pdf

Galbraith, J. K. (2009). *The great crash 1929*. Reprint. Boston: Mariner.

Gever, J., Kaufmann, R., & Skole, D. (1991). *Beyond oil: The threat to food and fuel in the coming decades*. 3rd ed. Ed. C. Vorosmarty. Boulder, Colorado: University Press of Colorado.

Gibbons, E. (1964). *Stalking the blue-eyed scallop*. New York: David McKay.

Goodchild, P. (1999). *Survival skills of the North American Indians*. 2nd ed. Chicago: Chicago Review Press.

Gordon, R. B., Bertram, M., & Graedel, T. E. (2006, January 31). *Metal stocks and sustainability*. Retrieved from www.mindfully.org/Sustainability/2006/Metal-Stocks-Gordon31jan06.htm

Green, D. G., Grove, E., & Martin, N. A. (2005). *Crime and civil society: Can we become a more law-abiding people?* London: Civitas: Institute for the Study of Civil Society. Retrieved from www.civitas.org.uk/pdf/cs36.pdf

Greider, W. (1998). *One world, ready or not: The manic logic of global capitalism*. New York: Simon and Schuster.

Grove, N. (1974, June). Oil, the dwindling treasure. *National Geographic*. Retrieved from www.hubbertpeak.com/hubbert/natgeog.htm

Hall, C. (2008, April 15). Unconventional oil: Tar sands and shale oil—EROI on the Web, Part 3 of 6. *The Oil Drum*. Retrieved from www.theoildrum.com/node/3839

Hanson, J. (1999, Spring). Energetic limits to growth. *Energy*. Retrieved from www.dieoff.org/page175.htm

Hardin, G. (1968). The tragedy of the commons. *Science*, 162. Retrieved from http://dieoff.org/page95.htm

Hardin, G. (1995). *Living within limits: Ecology, economics, and population taboos*. New York: Oxford University Press.

Harrabin, R. (2009, September 11). UK 'could face blackouts by 2016.' *BBC News*. Retrieved from http://news.bbc.co.uk/2/hi/science/nature/8249540.stm

Harris, M. (1989). *Our kind: Who we are, where we came from, where we are going*. New York: Harper Perennial.

Heinberg, R. (2009). *Blackout*. Gabriola Island, British Columbia: New Society.

Heinberg, R. (2010, May). China's coal bubble . . . and how it will deflate U.S. efforts to develop "clean coal." *MuseLetter* #216. Retrieved from http://richardheinberg.com/216-chinas-coal-bubble-and-how-it-will-deflate-u-s-efforts-to-develop-clean-coal

Hirsch, R. L. (2005, October). The inevitable peaking of world oil production. *Atlantic Council Bulletin 16* (3). Retrieved from http://321energy.com/editorials/hirsch/hirsch102205.html

Hoffer, E. (1989). *The true believer: Thoughts on the nature of mass movements*. New York: HarperPerennial.

Höök, M., & Aleklett, K. (2009, May 1). Historical trends in American coal production and a possible future outlook. *International Journal of Coal Geology*. Retrieved from www.sciencedirect.com/science/article/pii/S0166516209000317

Höök, M., Zittel, W., Schindler, J., & Aleklett, K. (2010, June 8). *Global coal production outlooks based on a logistic model*. Retrieved from www.sciencedirect.com/science/article/pii/S0016236110002954

Hubbert, M. K. (1956). *Nuclear energy and the fossil fuels*. American Petroleum Institute. Retrieved from www. hubbertpeak.com/hubbert/1956/1956.pdf

IPCC (Intergovernmental Panel on Climate Change). (2000). Special report on emissions scenarios. Retrieved from www.ipcc.ch/pdf/special-reports/spm/sres-en.pdf

IPCC (Intergovernmental Panel on Climate Change). (2007). Climate change 2007. Contribution of Working Group I to the Fourth Assessment Report of the Intergovernmental Panel on Climate Change. Retrieved from www.ipcc.ch/publications_ and_data/ar4/wg1/en/contents.html

Kaplan, R. D. (1994, February). The coming anarchy: How scarcity, crime, overpopulation, tribalism, and disease are rapidly destroying the social fabric of our planet. *The Atlantic Monthly*. Retrieved from www.theatlantic.com/magazine/ archive/1994/02/the-coming-anarchy/4670/

Kaplan, R. D. (2001). *The ends of the Earth: From Togo to Turkmenistan, from Iran to Cambodia—a journey to the frontiers of anarchy*. Gloucester, Massachusetts: Peter Smith Publisher.

Keynes, J. M. (1952). *Essays in persuasion*. London: Rupert Hart-Davis.

Kharecha, P. A., & Hansen, J. E. (2007, April 26). Implications of "peak oil" for atmospheric CO_2 and climate. Retrieved from http://arxiv.org/ftp/arxiv/papers/0704/0704.2782.pdf

King, F. H. (n.d.). *Farmers of forty centuries*. Emmaus, Pennsylvania: Organic Gardening.

Klare, M. T. (2002). *Resource wars: The new landscape of global conflict*. New York: Henry Holt and Company.

Knies, G. (2006). *Global energy and climate security through solar power from deserts*. Mediterranean Renewable Energy Cooperation in Co-operation with the Club of Rome. Retrieved from www.desertec.org/downloads/deserts_en.pdf

Kolankiewicz, L., & Beck, R. (2001, April). *Forsaking fundamentals: The U.S. environmental movement abandons U.S. population stabilization*. Washington, D.C.: Center for Immigration Studies. Retrieved from www.cis.org/sites/cis.org/files/articles/2001/forsaking/ forsaking.pdf

Kropotkin, P. (1968). *Memoirs of a revolutionist*. New York: Horizon.

Lappé, F. M. (1991). *Diet for a small planet*. New York: Ballantine.

Larsen, J. (2005, June 22). Wild fish catch hits limits—Oceanic decline offset by increased fish farming. Eco-Economy Indicators: Fish Catch. Earth Policy Institute. Indicators. Retrieved from www.earth-policy.org/indicators/C55/ fish_2005

Lee, R. B. (1968). What hunters do for a living, or, How to make out on scarce resources. In R. B. Lee and I. DeVore, eds., *Man the hunter*. Chicago: Aldine Publishing. Retrieved from http://artsci.wustl.edu/~anthro/articles/lee_1968_1.pdf

Leopold, J. (2006, October 17). Dark days ahead. *Truth Out*. Retrieved from www.truth-out.org/archive/item/66198: jason-leopold--dark-days-ahead

Logsdon, G. (1977). *Small-scale grain raising*. Emmaus, Pennsylvania: Rodale.

Lovelock, J. (2007, September 6). Respect the earth. *World Nuclear News*. Retrieved from www.world-nuclear-news.org/newsarticle.aspx?id=13998

Macalister, T. (2009, November 9). Key oil figures were distorted by US pressure, says whistleblower. *Guardian*. Retrieved from www.guardian.co.uk/environment/2009/nov/09/peak-oil-international-energy-agency

Martin, H., & Schumann, H. (1997). *The global trap: Civilization & the assault on democracy & prosperity*. Trans. Patrick Camiller. New York: St. Martin's Press.

Mason, M. K. (2010). *Housing: Then, now, and future*. Retrieved from www.moyak.com/papers/house-sizes.html

McChesney, R. (2004). *The problem of the media: US communication politics in the twenty-first century*. New York: Monthly Review Press.

McMahon, K. (2006, August 21). Remember, remember the 5th of September, 2000. *Peak Oil Blues*. Retrieved from www.peakoilblues.org/blog/2006/08/21/remember-remember-the-5th-of-september-2000/

Mercer Human Resource Consulting. (2006). Global/world cost of living rankings 2006. Retrieved from www.finfacts.ie/costofliving2006.htm

Mygatt, E. (2006, July 26). World's water resources face mounting pressure. *Eco-Economy Indicators*. Retrieved from www.earth-policy.org/index.php?/indicators/C57

Nelson, R. K. (1973). *Hunters of the northern forest: designs for survival among the Alaskan Kutchin*. Chicago: University of Chicago Press.

NERC (North American Electric Reliability Corporation). (2008). *Long-term reliability assessment 2008-2017*. Retrieved from www.nerc.com/files/LTRA2008v1_2.pdf

Oil Drum. (2010, February 4). World oil capacity to peak in 2010 says Petrobras CEO. *The Oil Drum*. Retrieved from www.theoildrum.com/node/6169

Orlov, D. (2005). *Post-Soviet lessons for a post-American century*. Retrieved from http://docs.google.com/Doc?id=dtxqwqr_20dc52sm

Oxford University. (2010, March 23). Oxford report: World oil reserves at tipping point. *Energy Bulletin*. Retrieved from www.energybulletin.net/node/52093

Petrole. (2010, March 25). Washington considers a decline of world oil production as of 2011. Retrieved from http://petrole.blog.lemonde.fr/2010/03/25/washington-considers-a-decline-of-world-oil-production-as-of-2011

Phleps, H. (1989). *The craft of log building*. Reprint. New York: HarperCollins.

Pimentel, D. (1984). *Energy flows in agricultural and natural ecosystems*. CIHEAM (International Centre for Advanced Mediterranean Agronomic Studies). Retrieved from http://om.ciheam.org/om/pdf/s07/CI010841.pdf

Pimentel, D., & Hall, C. W., eds. (1984). *Food and energy resources*. Orlando, Florida: Academic Press.

Pimentel, D., & Pimentel, M. H. (2007). *Food, energy, and society*. 3rd ed. Boca Raton, Florida: CRC Press.

Rau, C. (1884). *Prehistoric fishing in Europe and North America*. Smithsonian Contributions to Knowledge, 25. Washington.

Rifkin, J. (1995). *The end of work: The decline of the global labor force and the dawn of the post-market era*. New York: Tarcher/Putnam.

Riley, N. E. (2004, June). China's population: New trends and challenges. Population Reference Bureau. *Population Bulletin, 59* (2). Retrieved from www.prb.org/Source/59.2ChinasPopNewTrends.pdf

Roberts, J. M. (1992). *History of the world*. Rev. ed. Oxford: Helicon.

Roper, L. D. (2012, January 27). Minerals depletion. Retrieved from www.roperld.com/science/minerals/minerals.htm

Rostlund, E. (1952). *Freshwater fish and fishing in native North America*. University of California Publications in Geography, 9.

Salisbury, H. E. (2003). *The 900 days: The siege of Leningrad*. Cambridge, Massachusetts: Da Capo Press.

Schor, J. B. (1991). *The overworked American: The unexpected decline of leisure*. New York: HarperCollins.

Schumacher, E. F. (1989). *Small is beautiful: Economics as if people mattered*. New York: Harper & Row.

Simmons, M. R. (2006). *Twilight in the desert: The coming Saudi oil shock and the world economy*. Hoboken, New Jersey: John Wiley & Sons.

Smil, V. (2009, September 17). The iron age & coal-based coke: A neglected case of fossil-fuel dependence. *Master Resource*. Retrieved from http://masterresource.org/2009/09/a-forgotten-case-of-fossil-fuel-dependence-the-iron-age-requires-carbon-based-energy-like-it-or-not

Smith, D., & Vivekananda, J. (2007, November). A climate of conflict: The links between climate change, peace and war. *International Alert*. Retrieved from www.international-alert.org/sites/default/files/publications/A_climate_of_conflict.pdf

Smith, R. (2009, June 8). US foresees a thinner cushion of coal. *Wall Street Journal*. Retrieved from http://online.wsj.com/article/SB124414770220386457.html

Solomon, S. (1993). *Water-wise vegetables*. Seattle: Sasquatch.

Soros, G. (1998). *The crisis of global capitalism: Open society endangered*. New York: Public Affairs.

Spiedel, J. J., Sinding, S., Gillespie, D., Maguire, E., & Neuse, M. (2009, January). *Making the case for US international family planning assistance*. US Agency for International Development. Retrieved from www.jhsph.edu/gatesinstitute/_pdf/publications/MakingtheCase.pdf

Starr, C. G. (1991). *A history of the ancient world*. 4th ed. New York: Oxford University Press.

Stewart, H. (1977). *Indian fishing: Early methods on the Northwest Coast*. Vancouver: Douglas and McIntyre.

Storm van Leeuwen, J. W. (2008, February). *Nuclear power—the energy balance*. Retrieved from www.stormsmith.nl

Thurow, L. C. (1996). *The future of capitalism: How today's economic forces shape tomorrow's world*. New York: William Morrow.

Tresemer, D. (1981). *The scythe book*. Brattleboro, Vermont: Hand & Foot.

UN Environment Program. (2007). *Global environment outlook 4*. Retrieved from www.unep.org/geo/GEO4/report/GEO-4_Report_Full_en.pdf

US Census Bureau. (2012). Historical income tables—families. US Government Printing Office. Retrieved from www.census.gov/hhes/www/income/data/historical/families

USGS. (United States Geological Service) (2005). *Historical statistics for mineral and material commodities in the United States*. Data Series 140. Retrieved from http://minerals.usgs.gov/ds/2005/140/

Weatherwax, P. (1954). *Indian corn in old America*. New York: Macmillan.

Wheat, M. M. (1967). *Survival arts of the primitive Paiutes*. Reno: University of Nevada Press.

Youngquist, W. (2000, October). Alternative energy sources. *Oil Crisis*. Retrieved from www.hubbertpeak.com/youngquist/altenergy.htm

Youngquist, W. (2008). *Geodestinies: The inevitable control of earth resources over nations and individuals*. 2nd ed. Portland, Oregon: National Book Company, Education Research Associates.